D1029694

JAN GORAK

THE ALIEN MIND
OF RAYMOND WILLIAMS

A LITERARY FRONTIERS EDITION, NO. 32

UNIVERSITY OF MISSOURI PRESS

COLUMBIA, 1988

Copyright © 1988 by
The Curators of the University of Missouri
University of Missouri Press, Columbia, Missouri 65211
Printed and bound in the United States of America

Library of Congress Cataloging-in-Publication Data

Gorak, Jan, 1952–
        The alien mind of Raymond Williams / Jan Gorak

        (A Literary Frontiers Edition)
        Bibliography: p.
        ISBM 0–8262–0688–3
        1. Williams, Raymond—Criticism and interpretation.
I. Title. II. Series.
PR6073/I4329Z67   1988
828'.91409—dc19   88–4812

∞™ This paper meets the minimum requirements of
the American National Standard for Permanence of Paper
for Printed Library Materials, Z39.48, 1984.

TO IRENE

CONTENTS

I. INTRODUCTION

F ROM his first public appearance as an editor of *Politics and Letters* and *The Critic* in 1946 to his death in 1988, Raymond Williams built up a prodigious and versatile repertoire, appearing as a literary critic, culture critic, theorist, Marxist, dramatist, scriptwriter, television broadcaster, novelist, poet, political pundit, media analyst, Welsh nationalist, and popular moralist. During the 1980s, sales of his books topped the one million mark in Britain alone. Yet behind his apparently endless series of masks, Williams remained a difficult figure for the reader to grasp. He lacked the verbal ingenuity of Christopher Ricks, another British academic who enjoys access to the airwaves, yet he seemed unwilling to employ Marxist categories as remorselessly as his fellow leftists in *New Left Review*. His own prose appears dense, sometimes opaque, without the elegance of Frank Kermode or the geniality of Denis Donoghue. Although he wrote as much critical journalism as any of those writers, and in publications as diverse, his self-presentation as his generation's perplexed, troubled, radical conscience denied him the succès de scandale of E. P. Thompson or Christopher Hill. Indeed, judging from correspondence on file at the British Broadcasting Corporation, his attempts to secure a wider audience for his social diagnoses met with limited success. Not for Williams the popular notoriety of media socialists such as J. B. Priestley, A. J. P. Taylor, or, from an earlier period, George Bernard Shaw.

Moreover, Williams consistently defined himself in opposition to the labels that seem conveniently to represent his own position. Do his wide-ranging general interests and his persistent evaluative thrust mark him as a "Cambridge critic," the latest in a dynasty stretching from Leslie Stephen to F. R. Leavis? Or does his career of forty years offer a long and often oblique debate with

1

Marxism? Williams himself vehemently rejected the first speculation. On the contrary, in Ronald Hayman's *My Cambridge*, he emphasized his estrangement from British university culture. "It was not my Cambridge. That was clear from the beginning. I have now spent eighteen years in the university, in three distinct periods. In each of them I have started by being surprised to be there, and then, in time, made some kind of settlement. But this has always, even in the longest period, felt temporary."[1] It is significant that while Leavis remained at Cambridge until the year before his seventieth birthday, Williams took early retirement in 1983. Clearly, one can get only so much mileage from viewing him as a traditional British culture critic. The young Williams certainly read exceptionally closely the work of Arnold, T. S. Eliot, Orwell, Hoggart, Leavis, and the *Scrutiny* group, but to understand even an early work like *Culture and Society* (1958) one must trace how far its author deviates from cultural conceptions that were popular between the 1930s and the 1950s. Although his work contains many echoes of the Scrutineers, Williams, unlike Leavis, consciously reshaped the work of the culture critic to meet the needs of what he called "this unprecedented dislocating mobile society."[2]

Can one, then, leave Williams to the attentions of the radical left, who in the 1970s and 1980s have taken by far the most intimate interest in his career? To see him as a Marxist would have the benefit of convenience, since a clear line could then be drawn between the work up to *The Country and the City* (1973), in which Williams is a deeply interested but nonaligned observer of Marxism, and the subsequent work, in which his affiliations to a revolutionary position become uncompromisingly overt. But even in the later period, there remains the difficulty of estimating the nature of his commitment. Is Williams an intellectual Marxist like the Frederic Jameson of *Marxism and Form*? Is he an ideological Marxist like the Lukács of *The Meaning of Contemporary Realism*? Or is he perhaps a Marxist demagogue, popularizing and disseminating his creed for the predominantly youthful audience targeted by Terry Eagleton in *Marxism and Literary Criticism*?

In *Marxism and Literature* (1977), Williams spoke of his discovery of a European Marxist intelligentsia—Gramsci, Goldmann, Althusser, Bloch, and Benjamin—that gave him "the sense, for the first time in my life, of belonging to a sphere and dimension of *work* in which I could feel at home." Yet as he also admitted in the same work, his basic intellectual method involves "long and often internal and solitary debate."[3] His most lengthy, controversial, and widely reported debate occurred, of course, with Marxism itself. Just two years after *Marxism and Literature*, in the afterword to a 1979 reissue of *Modern Tragedy* (1966), Williams qualified his revolutionary Marxism by confessing an ineradicable attachment to British culture and society. "At the slow turning point of a culture like my own, in the very cultures that are the rich expressions of this lived and now dying order, our feelings are necessarily more intricate and more involved. . . . In our relations with others . . . we have been more effectively incorporated into the deepest structures of this now dying order than it was ever, while it was strong, our habit to think or even suspect."[4] So deep an attachment to an admittedly "dying order" would sound odd on the lips of Perry Anderson or Christopher Hill. Indeed, the very ambivalence of Williams's hostilities and commitments—his insertion of this baffled afterword into one of his most militant works, his ability to sound like Leavis even as he identifies himself with a band of far more radical continental theorists—runs counter to an interpretation of his works in terms of his loyalties to a single party line.

It is perhaps the "intricacy" and "involvement" of his feelings that complicated Williams's relationship with organized left-wing politics. His official affiliation with the Communist party was exceedingly brief, over a period of months rather than years in the late 1930s. He described his position after the war as "to the left of the Labour Party," but regarding the "British Communist Party as irrelevant because of the intellectual errors it had made"[5]—a position of impatience with the orthodox opposition and dissatisfaction with the status quo reminiscent of Gramsci and the young Lukács. For a brief period in the mid–1970s, Williams seemed willing to identify himself with a European Marxist intelligentsia. But his newfound faith suffered lightning qualification during the late 1970s and 1980s when the thinkers he had praised in earlier essays became subsumed in a succession of alienating methodologies. Reacting strongly against the "inherent distances and impersonalities"[6] of the new structuralist and poststructuralist systems, Williams frequently turned in his later works to a more radical populist style of impassioned address, so that the revised editions of books like *Modern Tragedy* (1979) and *Keywords* (1983) find him meditating for a by no means exclusively academic audience on the kind of traditional moral issues—hope, the future, speaking to each other—associated with Cobbett and Hoggart. It is in this guise, the angry but nonaligned cultural prophet, that in *Modern Tragedy* Williams spoke of "the slowly settling loss of any acceptable future" and of "a social model which is the last end of hope, for if we cannot, under any conditions, speak or try to speak fully to each other, that is the real end" (*MT*, 209, 215).

Intellectual, common man, Welsh proletarian, European Marxist, theater critic, novelist, media pundit: during his long and varied career, Williams privately absorbed and publicly repudiated a series of roles and affiliations, with fascinating consequences for his style and sensibility. On the one hand, his work betrays a humanist's attachment to the past, to regions of mind and private experience that force him into elegy, meditation, and reverie. On the other hand, his responsibility as a socialist to the future moves him toward a more programmatic, abstract mode of thinking. If socialist hope leads him to affirm "the conviction that men can direct their own lives, by breaking through the pressures and restrictions of older forms of society, and by discovering new common institutions,"[7] frank personal testimony registers nonetheless a "terrifying loss of connection" along with "men and women broken by the pressure to accept this as normal, and by the deferment and corrosion of hope and desire" (*MT*, 13). A third tension arises from his conviction, derived in part from Orwell, in part from his experiences with the Campaign for Nuclear Disarmament, that the future is literally unthinkable. One result is the savage prophecy he ventilates in *Towards 2000* (1983), where he shows how a world of advertising and electronic media closets the individual in a kind of ersatz mind-drama, "a vigorous spectacular and consumerist militarism."[8] As so often in the later Williams, the style and the thought are exactly matched. In the late 1970s and the 1980s, he increasingly preferred the rough-hewn phrasing of Orwell and Cobbett (to both of whom during this period he devoted books) to the abstractions of the academy on the one side or of the revolutionary left on the other.

Despite his reluctant endorsement of what he grimly termed the "short revolution" in a 1977 interview with *New Left Review* (*PL*, 420), Williams remained closer to R. H. Tawney than to Che Guevara. More often than not, he criticized the "dying order" on personal and ethical grounds, pointing to the "dislocating" quality of modern social and cultural life, and blaming intellectuals in particular for working "at a quite exceptional distance from the lives and relationships they address, so that what is reaching furthest into our common life has the mode of a stranger, even the profession of a stranger" (*WS*, 224). Yet he also admitted his own participation, as a Welshman, a Marxist, and a working-class Cambridge don, in the same pattern of alienation. The new "objective" disciplines in sociology, anthropology, aesthetics, and so on, he confessed to viewing

with the eyes of a stranger. . . . I can feel the bracing cold of their inherent distances and impersonalities and yet have to go on saying that they are indeed ice-cold. I see, practically and theoretically, the estranging consequences of the general assumption—as active in modernist literature as in theoretical linguistics and structuralist Marxism—that the systems of

5

human signs are generated within the systems themselves and that to think otherwise is a humanist error. (*WS*, 223)

For Williams, the mind consists of a web of inherited allegiances that modern methods of inquiry may not even register. This means that the dynamism he accepts as a cultural materialist is belied by the estrangement that oppresses him when he feels six centuries of British (and Welsh) history meet the full force of what he despairingly calls "the decisive culture of an international capitalist world" (*WS*, 223).

But Williams's deepest estrangement concerns that more local capitalist world located across his native border. As he told *New Left Review* in 1977, "If you look at the implied relationships of nearly all the books I have written, I have been arguing with what I take to be official English culture" (*PL*, 316). Where Leavis or L. C. Knights or the *Scrutiny* group regard "English" as the highest possible praise for a writer, Williams rarely uses the word without suspicion. In fact, he responds to "English" culture as an outsider, an inhabitant of a border country where "we could speak of both Welsh and English as foreigners" (*PL*, 26). Williams's examination of "official English culture" starts from a deep-rooted antagonism; he confronts that culture rather than celebrates it.

If England functions for Williams as the enemy, then his native Wales provides conscience and consciousness. In *The Country and the City,* he confessed, "The only landscape I ever see, in dreams, is the Black Mountain village in which I was born." Williams felt in his Welsh origins the strength of a lasting attachment to the kind of vividly realized social and moral order he called a "knowable community." He recalled, "When I go back to that country, I feel a recovery of a particular kind of life, which appears, at times, as an inescapable identity, a more positive connection than I have known elsewhere. Many other men feel this, of their own native places, and the strength of the idea of settlement, old and new, is then positive and unquestioned."[9] Yet Wales enjoys an ambivalent status in

Williams's scheme of things, for, as the site of "settlement," it embodies two conflicting ideas. On the one hand, "settlement" suggests the local ties that men and women forge virtually unconsciously in childhood. On the other hand, it suggests his commitment to a less spontaneous, more consciously structured form of radical social reorganization, a postrevolutionary negotiation of group responsibilities and rights.

But for the most part, Williams did not labor this contradiction, since his whole life as a creative writer depended on Wales for its nourishment. In his novels *Border Country* (1960) and *Second Generation* (1964), Wales supplies the link with the past that renews the strength of the respective protagonists, allowing them to begin again the struggle to reshape the future that fuels the third part of the trilogy, *The Fight for Manod* (1979). In "A Letter from the Country," a play that appeared on BBC television in 1966, the decency and idealism of Wales set a marker for the Labour party's ethical decline, its unwillingness in office to honor the promises from which its political legitimacy derived. On the one side, then, Wales carries for Williams the charge of a symbolic land invested with affection, nostalgia, and loyalty.

On the other side, however, Wales plays a very different but equally important role. After he acknowledged its symbolic part in underwriting his more utopian convictions—his hopes that a "short revolution" would blast a decaying social order into renewal along radically egalitarian lines—Williams went on to describe it as the place where he learned his hardest political lesson. For the crucial problem about Wales was that he had to leave it.

> The problem has always been, for most people, how to go on living where they are. I know this also personally: not only because I had to move out for an education . . . but because the whole region in which I was born has been steadily and terribly losing its people, who can no longer make a living there. When I hear the idealisation of settlement, I do not need to borrow the first feelings; I know, in just that sense, what

neighbourhood means, and what is involved in separation and leaving. But I know, also, why people have had to move, why so many moved in my own family. So that I then see the idealisation of settlement, in its ordinary literary-historical version, as an insolent indifference to most people's needs. (CC, 84)

It is not surprising that the first study of Williams should have appeared in a series called "Writers of Wales." Not surprising, but not entirely accurate either. For in Wales, he learned one of the most bitterly estranging facts about modern life, the mobility that in *The English Novel from Dickens to Lawrence* (1970) he repeatedly described as "unprecedented," and that generated new literary and cultural forms by virtue of its novelty. Williams's national and class origins made him view these cultural forms with suspicion. As a regional intellectual alienated from his own region, he spoke of the term *British* in the way of his ancestors, as one "not used much, except by people one distrusted" (PL, 26). Much of his career represents a Welshman's examination of an alien British culture, an examination conducted by a man separated, by training and circumstances, from his own native land. For these reasons, therefore, I shall suggest that alienation, rather than national or doctrinal affiliation, supplies the key by which Williams can be unlocked.

* * *

In *Keywords*, Williams calls alienation "one of the most difficult words in the language," adding that "in its evidence of extensive feeling of a division between *man* and *society*, it is a crucial element in a very general structure of meanings."[10] *Alienation* is in fact a word with a very long history. In the fourteenth century, it carried a theological charge that by the next century had become more secular. For Wycliffe, *alienation* signified estrangement from God, while for Lydgate the word marked a transfer of property. However, the idea gathers most of its

8

modern connotations in the late eighteenth and early nineteenth centuries, a period Williams identifies with a revolution in social semantics, in which words like *culture, art, genius,* and *personality* all took on their distinctive modern meanings. Hegel's *Phenomenology of Mind* (1807) presents the development of culture and state power as an estrangement from the objective mind, while Feuerbach's *The Essence of Christianity* (1841) views religion as an alienating power that diverts the nobler qualities of the species to a God who serves as a sublimated projection of man's own deepest instincts. Marx's early *Economic and Philosophic Manuscripts of 1844* consolidates and expands on Feuerbach's model by presenting alienation as the product of a market economy that separates the laborer from his fruits. Common to all these analyses is the sense of a sovereign human destiny that in the contingencies of civil and economic existence becomes estranged from its true potential. It is not surprising, then, that *alienation* becomes perhaps the key concept in the attempt to construct a humanist Marx, a Marx less concerned with legislating the route toward a scientific socialism than with alerting humanity to the existential dilemmas it faces as a citizen, believer, and producer.

The conviction that human beings had sold themselves cheap in the worship of the state or in the market proved indispensable for Marxist and radical writers who, from Lukács onward, tried to steer socialism away from its Stalinist sponsors. Many of these writers, like Williams himself, belonged to ethnic or racial minorities, the author of *History and Class Consciousness* being only the first of a succession of modern Jewish writers to deploy the idea. In the 1940s, American Jewish intellectuals like Nathan Glazer and Irving Howe put alienation at the center of their analyses of the marginalized young man of ideas, estranged alike from family pieties and a lowbrow popular culture. In 1956, Erich Fromm's *The Sane Society* mounted a fervent moral and religious critique of American capitalism in terms of its pathological effect on the personality, while C. Wright Mills's *The Sociological Imag-*

9

ination (1959) presented alienation as the occupational hazard of the postwar intellectual. In *The End of Ideology* (1960), Daniel Bell neatly reversed Mills's point by suggesting that the concept of alienation allowed American socialists to analyze their societies with a refinement unattainable by the orthodox Soviet Marxist . For Bell, alienation provided a way of accepting a Marxist diagnosis while stopping short of a Marxist prescription, for by focusing on the troubled mind of the socialist intellectual, he defused the explosive potential of Marxist thinking. But for both Mills and Bell, the intellectual, shorn of his traditional loyalties, and without a role in a society increasingly geared to spectacle and conformity, seemed the apogee of modern alienation.

Given his affiliations with the non-Soviet left and his affection for the dying humanist order, it is surprising that Williams never confronts the idea of alienation at length. As a Welshman he belonged to an ethnic minority in England, while his working-class status in an emphatically middle-class university marginalized him still further. But for all his silence on the issue, alienation is constantly at the margins of his work, gathering momentum over the course of his career, and in effect becoming the hidden theme behind his prolonged interrogation of English culture. As the following pages will suggest, the concept of alienation helps to locate the buried matter of Williams's work and also explains his peculiarities of manner. Constantly drawn by the desire to revisit old obsessions, to work through his own estrangements by an interrogation of an alien culture's monuments, beset by a compulsion to test the authenticity of his own responses, forever seeking to identify "the real" shape of a situation or problem, Williams offers a case study in the psychology and methods of the alienated intellectual.

In fact, Williams's career goes far toward proving that alienation cuts deepest into the man who most comprehensively surveys it, the intellectual himself. At each stage of Williams's career, whether he is playing the theater critic as a young man, the culture and society man in his early maturity, or then, in breathtaking succession, media analyst, Marxist, novelist, and prophet, alienation serves as his *éminence grise,* dictating his procedures and shaping his conclusions. His alienation from postwar British theater inspired his first widely reviewed books, the studies of European naturalism undertaken in *Drama from Ibsen to Eliot* (1952), *Drama in Performance,* and *Preface to Film* (both 1954). A larger alienation involving a whole series of postwar events—the failure of the Labour government between 1945 and 1951, the internecine socialist battles behind the collapse of his journal *Politics and Letters* (1947–1948), the hegemonic redefinition of cultural matters attempted in T. S. Eliot's *Notes towards the Definition of Culture* (1948), his personal insecurities as a teacher from the wrong side of the class line—all these experiences left Williams feeling powerless and blocked. The death of *Politics and Letters* dealt a particular blow, for this represented his sustained bid to "unite radical left politics with Leavisite literary criticism" (*PL,* 65). As he told *New Left Review* in 1977, the folding of the journal left him shattered.

> The collapse of the periodical was a personal crisis for me. So many other initiatives, like the film, had also been blocked or failed. . . . For a period I was in such a state of fatigue and withdrawal that I stopped reading papers or listening to the news. At that point, apart from going on with the actual adult education teaching, I felt I could only write myself out of this in a non-collaborative way. I pulled back to do my own work. For the next ten years I wrote in nearly complete isolation. (*PL,* 77)

The completeness of that isolation taxes belief. In the immediate postwar period, Williams wrote *Drama from Ibsen to Eliot* (1952) as a reconstruction of the history of the naturalist theater, convinced that such a work would be "the most important piece of scholarship our dramatic literature could receive."[11] Yet Eric Bentley's *The Modern Theatre* had appeared in 1946, covering very similar material and written out of almost identical convictions. Both writers are appalled by the contemporary debasements of naturalism in the commercial theater. Both devote many pages to Ibsen, often picking the same passages for analysis. And, most important of all, both extend to drama the kind of detailed attention previously reserved for lyric poetry.

In the same way, Williams wrote *Culture and Society* (1958) in ignorance of Richard Hoggart's *The Uses of Literacy* (1957) and E. P. Thompson's *The Making of the English Working Class* (1963), both in preparation during this period. Nor did this isolation have the ten-year limit Williams himself assigns to it. During the 1960s, he continued to work by himself, producing both *The Long Revolution* (1961) and *Communications* (1962) without noticing European and American developments that were turning media studies into an independent discipline. Despite his origins in a densely structured working-class community, Williams approaches his host of topics as a polemical private researcher, advancing his own individual thesis with a heady disregard for competing—or even supporting—documentation. As he himself admitted in 1978, he prepared his Cambridge lectures on the English novel not as "a professional literary scholar" but as someone "quite out of touch" (*PL*, 243). Williams instinctively claimed independence from existing sources. It was as if he must feel utterly isolated in order to work at all, so strident were his claims for independence from even the most elementary source.

Indeed, Williams's greatest source of intellectual development was probably Williams. In the immediate postwar period, youthful ambition led him to launch a periodical and a press, to outline a film, and to write a novel. The failure of each of these projects drove him back to an earlier obsession, the Ibsen "who spoke nearest to my sense of my own condition at the time" (*PL*, 62). "At the time": again Williams understated the almost compulsive repetition in his character and in his career. Ibsen, the artist of alienated exile, provided more than the temporary refuge that Williams implies, for his quarrel with the conventions of naturalism stretched across half a dozen books and nearly twenty five years. For instance, one of the issues that exercised him in his early work on the drama was the meaning of the word *neighbor.* Yet in 1973, nearly thirty years after a Cambridge lecture where he first argued with L. C. Knights and Wolf Mankowitz about the meaning of the term, he reopens the debate in the pages of *The Country and the City* (1973).

Another almost obsessive topic is George Orwell, whom he anatomizes as the representative modern man, alienated and estranged. Orwell provides the subject for a climactic chapter in *Culture and Society,* a monograph in 1971, a volume of *Twentieth Century Views* in 1974, and a 1984 revision of the earlier monograph. Beyond Orwell's empirical, matter-of-fact style, Williams identifies an essential imposture, "an isolated writer exposed to a suffering but unconnecting world. The need to intervene, to force active connections, is the road away from Wigan Pier, back to an indifferent and sleepy and uncaring world, which has to be told about the isolation and the suffering."[12] In Orwell's very social mobility—his successive incarnations as policeman, convalescent, soldier, intellectual, and writer—Williams detects not a gentleman's virtuosity but an exile's alienation, a sense of relationships as "characteristically meagre, ephemeral, reluctant, disillusioning, even betraying" (O, 89). And when he goes on to describe this as the sensibility of the outsider, he returns to the subject that launched his career as a dramatic critic, in an essay on James Joyce's *Exiles* published in *Politics and Letters* in 1948. In effect, he reworks the theme of exile in Joyce and Orwell through the whole course of his career, from *Culture and Society* in 1958 to *The Country and the City* in 1973 to *Towards 2000* in 1983.

But sometimes Williams did not trouble himself even to rework his material, so that early work turns up in later books as an unmolded foreign presence. The discussions of Austen, George Eliot, Dickens, Hardy, and Lawrence that form part of *The English Novel from Dickens to Lawrence* (1971) reappear in *The Country and the City* published just two years later. Eighteen years after undertaking an analysis of "Britain in the Sixties" in *The Long Revolution* (1961), Williams reprints the same analysis as part of *Towards 2000* (1979). Similarly, in *Problems in Materialism and Culture* (1980), he counters those who see a pre- and post-Marxist Williams by reprinting essays as far apart as the 1950s and the late 1970s.

These repetitions perhaps represent his bid to reaffirm the integrity of the initial investigation, to underscore the authenticity of his credentials as a writer. Yet the cumulative force of his evidence is that integrity cannot exist in a world that appears as a host of divisions between classes, families, and generations. For as he concedes in the last pages of *The Country and the City,* the ultimate division lies elsewhere: "The last recess of the division of labour is this recess within ourselves, where what we want and what we believe we can do seem impassably divided." To most critics, so radical a division would seem impossible to heal. But for Williams it is easy, for with a typical heedlessness to the actual proofs, he immediately asserts, "We can overcome division only by refusing to be divided. That is a personal decision but then a social action" (*CC*, 306). The swing between pessimism and utopianism is all too frequent in his prose, undercutting his emphasis—surprising for a socialist—on the individual will. In fact, his interiorized version of the Marxist dialectic carries contradictions that only an intensely meditative writer would have the patience to explore, and even then only through a range of genres and approaches. Williams's early choice of occupation and role condemned him, for more than forty years, to confront and to defeat that most basic of all divisions, the division within the alienated self. The various fronts on which he attacked this "breach in nature" will suggest the divisions between the sections that follow.

II. DRAMA

THE majority of Williams's commentators agree that his dramatic interests remain difficult to place in the light of his work as a whole. Terry Eagleton, noting that "a volume of dramatic criticism has regularly punctuated his production of 'social' texts," confesses that "the relations between the two bodies of work are not easy to decipher." J. P. Ward, who finds "something undramatic in his dramatic preoccupations," sees Williams as a thoroughly academic critic, despite his interest in the drama as performance and social experience. "There is an atmosphere of 'Cambridge English' in his two books of dramatic criticism, with their congested textual examination." When Stuart Hampshire and Frank Kermode submitted their very different assessments of *Modern Tragedy* (1966), they shared a belief that the book was scarcely dramatic criticism. Hampshire described it as "imaginative sociology" and "gentle, sincere, discursive meditation—almost a spiritual autobiography." Kermode acknowledged its ambitious bid to make a "genuine connection with a life-work in history of ideas, criticism, and fiction," but he attacked its swerve from autobiography to doctrine, its desertion of its experiential opening for the ideological program advanced at its core.[1]

It is not easy to understand why an intelligence as abstract and ruminative as Williams's should occupy itself with the drama. To discover that the young Wallace Stevens supported himself in summer vacations by working as a fairground barker might not tax belief much more. Williams turned to the theater partly by contingency, partly by design. His career does not have that pristine symmetry he sometimes ascribed to it; yet the drama does not form a separate enclave in an otherwise austere body of work. As a young critic with a reputation to earn, Williams looked to the drama to do pioneering work that lyric poetry, for instance, could not provide. Nor could lyric poetry explore the communal "structure of feeling" to which his criticism perpetually returns. In the drama, as in no other genre, an audience can see the shape of its common life and explore the limits of its own cohesion. In the drama, an author can imagine and test verifiable alternatives to everyday reality. It cannot have escaped Williams that the postwar British theater largely shirked these tests, choosing instead to combine a detailed reproduction of bourgeois life with intermittent, highly sensationalized escapes from it. It is scarcely surprising that a writer as interested in alienation as Williams, and beginning his career in conditions of theatrical crisis, should establish both an academic and a practical interest in the drama, for dramatic performance can reproduce alienation under laboratory conditions.

No critic has so far confronted the full range of Williams's achievement, which comprises five full-length studies (*Drama from Ibsen to Eliot* [1952], *Drama in Performance* [1954, revised 1968], *Preface to Film*, with Michael Orrom [1954], *Modern Tragedy* [1966, revised 1979], and *Drama from Ibsen to Brecht* [1968]), numerous essays, and three plays ("Koba" [1966], "A Letter from the Country" [1966], and "Public Inquiry" [1967]). Over a twenty-five-year period, Williams maintained an almost obsessive concern with naturalist drama. In 1947, when he made his debut as a dramatic critic as the author of "A Dialogue on Actors," published in the ill-fated journal *The Critic*, he revealed a passionate antipathy to the sensationalism that contemporary audiences accepted as naturalistic performance. Presenting the modern theater's "attempt at superficial verisimilitude" as a willingness to reduce the words of an author to a vehicle for star performance, he denounced naturalism as a genre inevitably at odds with itself. "By discarding all possible dramatic conventions an attempt is made to produce an immediate illusion of real life."[2] Williams's early work attacks naturalism at every level. In *Drama from Ibsen to Eliot*, he attacks its verbal impoverishment. In *Drama in Performance*, he pushes it to

16

the edge of mainstream European theater. In *Preface to Film,* he blocks its attempt to influence the growth of a new medium.

Williams's work up to *Modern Tragedy* shows an unwillingness to confront the naturalist drama on its own terms. In the "readings" he provides at this stage, even the greatest naturalist plays, *Ghosts* or *Lady Julie,* become alienated products devoted to the self-contradictory policy of dramatizing an "illusion of reality." In the later work, however, Williams arrives at a position more sympathetic to naturalist conventions. *Modern Tragedy* and *Drama from Ibsen to Brecht* (an expansion and substantial revision of *Drama from Ibsen to Eliot*) return to the same plays that he had earlier seen as lacking in verbal life and significant dramatic action. But now he sees the thin texture of these plays as an index to significant areas of alienation in modern life. At this stage, he finds a central tension in naturalist drama, between the individual's search for liberation and the social pressure toward conformity. In *Drama from Ibsen to Eliot,* he writes as a student of the Leavises and of T. S. Eliot; in *Drama from Ibsen to Brecht,* he writes as a student of the long revolution and as a militant socialist.

What remains astonishing, though, is how thoroughly the later book reworks the earlier seam. The pages of *Drama from Ibsen to Brecht* contain material composed as early as 1947 and as late as 1967. Its revisions of *Drama from Ibsen to Eliot* range from minor adjustments to major revaluations, with the discussion of Ibsen providing an example of the first, the sections on Chekhov and O'Casey examples of the last. In its tissue of multiple revision and its repeated meditation around a common core of touchstone texts, the work suggests a prolonged argument with the estrangements of middle-class existence, estrangements that are projected into the very furniture of the naturalist stage. As Williams told *New Left Review* in 1978,

The most powerful physical image created in the period of major naturalist drama is the living room as a trap. People look through the window to see what is happening in the world beyond, which cannot be shown. Messages come through the door from the world outside, but the centre of dramatic interest is inside. A passive sense of the environment, not merely as forming . . . but as totally determining . . . is eventually embodied in this immobile, trapped form. (*PL*, 205).

Throughout his career, Williams served as a critic of society by vocation and as a dramatist and dramatic critic by professional choice. His obsessive focus on the naturalist environment reflects his closeness to his own Welsh borderland and his corresponding hostility to an estranged and dehumanized capitalist world. In his mature work on the drama, he presents naturalism not so much as a superficial reproduction of bourgeois social life as a dramatized version of its essential alienation.

* * *

However, the angle of vision from which Williams attacked this alienation did not remained fixed. His early dramatic criticism views naturalism from above, from the lofty perspective of a sensibility cultivated by Cambridge, T. S. Eliot, I. A. Richards, and F. R. Leavis. Like these writers, he thinks that literary criticism carries a special mission to heal the divisions caused by the loss of a common culture and a common sensibility. Behind his first three books on the drama—*Drama in Performance, Drama from Ibsen to Eliot*, and *Preface to Film*—stand the powerful myths of dissociation promulgated by his predecessors, who saw the twentieth century as fatally bifurcated between thought and feeling, commerce and culture. Shadowing the pages of *Drama from Ibsen to Eliot* are the influential myths of crisis disseminated by Eliot and Leavis, which present the development of the modern world as a series of splits between science and myth, mechanism and organism. The upshot is an age polarized between mass and minority culture, a polarization that

Williams's early programmatic work *Reading and Criticism* (1950) tried to resolve by extending the reading habits of a Cambridge elite to a wider and more socially heterogeneous audience. A similar motive underlies his earliest dramatic work, which he defined unequivocally as "literary criticism . . . based on demonstrated judgments from texts, rather than on historical survey or generalised impressions: of the kind, that is to say, which is known in England as practical criticism."[3]

Williams's early work, in other words, reflects Cambridge training and Cambridge tastes. *Scrutiny's* concern with the role of the arts in a mechanized society made it natural for him to direct his attention to drama, since the immediate postwar period marked a boom in dramatic productions and the reappearance of some distinctive talents, with performers like John Gielgud, Laurence Olivier, Paul Scofield, Ralph Richardson, Edith Evans, Sybil Thorndike, and Peggy Ashcroft ensuring the success of established plays by Coward, Rattigan, and Priestley, and also helping to launch new talents like Peter Ustinov, Christopher Fry, John Whiting, and Williams's own friend, Wolf Mankowitz. Even so, the tacit conventions of Cambridge literary criticism determined the way Williams responded to this new cultural situation. Along with other Cambridge critics of the 1940s and the 1950s, Williams tried to extend the methods and values of the practical critic to the study of the social arts. These critics tried to judge cinema, theater, and journalism by the criteria governing, for instance, an article on *Macbeth*, a *Macbeth* that became not so much a character study in ambition as "a statement of evil," a work that had a "greater affinity with *The Waste Land* than with *The Doll's House*."[4]

By 1947, when Williams wrote his first dramatic essay, practical criticism had devised a set way of tackling the drama. Paradoxically, however, its critical methods remained inherently undramatic. The work of F. R. Leavis, L. C. Knights, and D. A. Traversi proceeds by a kind of abstract analysis that has little to do with conditions in a theater. Typically, these critics begin by isolating a theme and then drape around it the play's language, action, and characterization. In their view, a dramatist finds his themes in the great upheavals of the common realm or in the moral crises in the life of the individual. In exemplary careers of canonical authors a theme can be followed across the shape of a career, so that Traversi, for instance, traces Shakespeare's study of kingship from *Henry VI* to *King Lear.* The isolation of such a pattern, and its demonstration in the verbal texture of the individual work, became for the Cambridge critics the guarantee of "seriousness" in the drama. Running parallel to this intense concern with moral issues embodied in concrete language lay the historical judgment that modern drama marked an unarrestable decline from the peak achievement of the Elizabethans.

The fountainhead for many such judgments was, of course, T. S. Eliot, whose own dramatic essays exerted a considerable influence over the Cambridge critics. Eliot deplored the impulse to realism that vitiated even Shakespearean drama, since such impulses inevitably produced the "exact likeness to the reality which is perceived by the most commonplace mind."[5] After the Shakespeare of *Measure for Measure* the Galsworthy of *Justice* was not far to seek. Against this routine representation of everyday reality, Eliot promoted a verse drama that reached to the deepest core of human experience. "The human soul," Eliot reflected, "in intense emotion, strives to express itself in verse. . . . The tendency, at any rate, of prose drama is to emphasise the ephemeral and superficial; if we want to get at the permanent and universal we tend to express ourselves in verse." Because Eliot saw modern drama as the flawed result of a fatal "distinction between drama and literature,"[6] he offered few detailed commentaries on naturalist plays. His judgments bore fruit in the methods and the subject matter of his successors, who largely ignored any dramatic writing after the Restoration.

If Eliot himself paid little attention to naturalist drama, his eminence and influence proved decisive on those who did, as the abundance of approving references to "Mr. Eliot" in Williams's first books makes clear. Although he signaled his partial independence from Eliot by electing to study nineteenth-century drama, Williams remained locked within Eliot's guiding assumptions and values. Indeed, some of his judgments appear inexplicable without a knowledge of these prior affiliations. Given such knowledge, however, it is not surprising that he should rank *Brand* and *Peer Gynt* as Ibsen's greatest achievements; that he should attack Chekhov because he wrote dramas around idiosyncratic characters rather than around organized ideas; and that he should see in Shaw only "the great literary figure in a society which was largely uninterested in literature" (*DIE*, 138). Eliot's campaign in the service of verse drama underpins the first judgment; L. C. Knights's attack on the nineteenth-century preference for portraiture rather than for thematic organization underpins the second; while Q. D. Leavis's theory of a cultural schism that set highbrows against masses underpins the third.

In fact, the belief of Eliot and *Scrutiny* in the existence of a canonical group of authors and texts that secretes the experience of the race displaces the simple aim Williams described in "A Dialogue on Actors": to provide "a competent analysis of naturalism, with the record of its growth." None of Williams's early dramatic writings aspire to or achieve the impartiality of scholarly history. At this stage, Williams, like Eliot, is constitutionally hostile to naturalism, presenting it as "a desultory attempt to reproduce conversation. . . . An attempt at superficial verisimilitude."[7] Later in his career, he would launch an impassioned critique of "universalist" assumptions in literary criticism, which he saw as taking no account of the diversity of modern experience. But his own early criticism betrays a similar inflexibility, for at this stage he strives to identify a "core" at the heart of "the dramatic experience," a core he identifies with the playwright's words.

> I have considered the question of the nature of "character" and "action" in literature in some detail, because the fact that

character and action become substantial in dramatic performance is one of the main reasons for the denial of drama as a
literary form. Performance is the means of communication of
dramatic literature, and these main elements in it—which do
not seem to be literary at all—lead to the prejudice which we
are considering. And this has been particularly the case in the
naturalist drama, because these elements have been heavily
emphasised, while at the same time the element of language,
in which the literary existence of drama principally resides,
has been modified in such a way as to make it appear not to
exist at all. (*DIE*, 21)

Williams's immediate target is the drama of J. B. Priestley
and Noel Coward, whose words function as little more
than a set of cues for performance by a star who will attract the kind of popular audience that will secure the
play's box-office success. In such a drama, words inevitably lose their preeminence to spectacle and repartee, an
imbalance that Williams's criticism tries to redress. Yet,
arguably, all he can do is redistribute this imbalance,
since his own prejudices are similarly limiting. His bias in
favor of language goes unquestioned, since he proceeds
without considering whether his desire to provide "an
account of modern naturalist drama which is supported
by detailed analysis of several naturalist plays" (*DIE*, 12)
must inevitably be compromised by a critical procedure
designed to promote the cause of verse drama.

Any criticism that elevates language above character
and action instead of seeing all three as organically related will inevitably favor poetic drama, since poetry is
customarily viewed as the most organized form of language. Williams's *Drama from Ibsen to Eliot*, with its stated
preference for Elizabethan drama and for the plays of
Eliot and Yeats, necessarily falls into this trap. Like Eliot
and *Scrutiny*, Williams is essentially prescriptive. He
argues that language shapes the pattern of experience
enacted on stage and ought to govern the responses of an
audience. Yet when he compiles a list of "general prejudices" that undermine critical analysis of the drama, he
does not list the prejudice in favor of verse drama that

underlies his own critique of naturalism. Clearly, his procedure is not strictly logical, for he establishes only that words are the raw material of the drama, not that they govern it as its sovereign element.

Given Williams's stated procedures, the course of *Drama in Performance* and *Drama from Ibsen to Eliot* becomes predictable. After uncovering a general moral theme—vocation in Ibsen, identity in Strindberg—he then lights on a basic flaw in the work as a whole. Ibsen's *Rosmersholm*, for instance, shuffles between the "explicit figures of the drama and as it were summaries of the slowly realised figures of the novel" (*DIE*, 80). Because Chekhov lacks "the convention of impersonal analysis which . . . supplies richness in fictions," his dramas expire "in slogan and catchphrase" (*DIE*, 130-31). In the climactic episode of Pirandello's *Henry the Fourth*, Williams perceives an anagnorisis that "cannot come into dramatic speech" (*DIE*, 195) but must signal its importance through stage directions.

From these comments it is clear that he views naturalist theater as a reader. Unable to free himself from the limiting assumption that language provides all dramatic life, his commentaries often ignore the substance of the action, focusing instead on the inadequacies of the playwright's words. His comments on the climax of *Henry the Fourth* are representative. Conceding that the scene "is one of the greatest moments in the Pirandello theatre," he adds that "one has only to look at it to be reminded of Pirandello's limits, limits that were, in spite of his technical experiments, essentially naturalist. The drama, the reality, if you like, cannot be achieved in words" (*DIE*, 194-95). Yet Pirandello's great moment would not appear so anticlimactic performed by an actor on stage. Williams allows the actor only an instrumental role; he repeatedly emphasizes that the author's words must fix the conditions of the actor's performance.

In the same spirit, he cannot find any validity in the devices by which naturalist dramatists have invested their plays with a larger symbolic action. Williams can see in Ibsen's wild duck, Chekhov's seagull, and Pirandello's masks only the marks of an alienated theater that invests in things what an earlier drama embodied in words. In Chekhov's plays, "there is an air, as in Ibsen's *The Wild Duck*, of disintegration, which springs directly from this absence. A gap must be filled, and to the rescue, as before, comes the unifying pressure of a stage device of atmosphere. It is a poor compromise" (*DIE*, 130–31). Yet by reducing actors to mouthpieces and symbols to machinery, Williams does little more than elevate prejudice to principle. The faltering reticence of Pirandello's Henry hardly matches Othello's soaring grandiloquence, but if his words are tracked back to their situation and source they become entirely appropriate, for he has elected to live his life in a disguise that has turned into a fixed identity. Neither character nor situation supports the kind of language to be expected in a Shakespearean tragedy, where the hero's social identity, at least, attracts considerably more markers. By applying Leavisian criteria to literature that will not bear that kind of close verbal scrutiny, Williams alienates himself from the very canon he seeks to reexamine.

* * *

Williams's second wave of dramatic criticism rides on motives and allegiances very different from his first. Behind the early work stand two powerfully distorting influences from the immediate postwar period: the myth of a dissociation between mass society and minority culture advanced in Q. D. Leavis's *Fiction and the Reading Public* (1932); and the exclusory pattern of a "great tradition" traced in F. R. Leavis's book of that name. But during the 1960s, when he began to work on *Modern Tragedy*, Williams would construct his own set of canonical texts, drawing not on an academic model of cultural history but on his own personal and political experience. Moreover, in the twelve years between *Drama in Performance* in 1954 and *Modern Tragedy* in 1966, the meaning of "experience" would dramatically shift. In the early work "experience" was a value to be embodied in precise and proper language; in the later work "experience" becomes existential, the authentic record of a social class struggling against its own alienation.

In the 1950s, Williams subscribed to the Leavisian view that "experience" served as a sovereign guarantee of literary merit. Yet his own work bore little relation to his own experience as a working-class intellectual, a teacher in adult education, and an editor of the radical journal *Politics and Letters*. In *Drama from Ibsen to Eliot,* his interpretations rested on the succession of cultural crises that fixed the shape of literary history for Eliot and *Scrutiny. Modern Tragedy* and *Drama from Ibsen to Brecht* similarly derive their momentum from crisis, but the crises that provoke these books belong to history rather than to academic mythology. Even if one does not share Williams's convictions about the relationship between the industrial revolution and the naturalist drama, it is still impossible to dispute the existence of either of these. Because it draws on verifiable social and political history rather than on cultural myth, Williams's later work gains in critical and interpretative force.

In 1961, Williams returned to Cambridge as a lecturer in the English faculty and as a Fellow of Jesus College. He had spent the previous fifteen years as the Oxford University delegate to the Workers' Educational Association (WEA), where he had been responsible for adult education classes reaching from Staffordshire in the north to Sussex in the south. The shift back into the undergraduate curriculum came as something of a shock. He recalled how, learning of his special responsibilities for teaching the drama, he reviewed his old notes only to rewrite them entirely. "It was as if I went into the lecture room with the text of a chapter from *Drama from Ibsen to Eliot* in front of me, and came out with a text of a chapter from *Modern Tragedy*" (*PL*, 211). Williams describes this transformation in almost miraculous terms. Yet given the pattern of his experience with the WEA and his increasingly radical socialist stance, a disenchantment with Eliot and *Scrutiny* would seem inevitable. He wrote his early work as a recent convert to high culture, eager to disseminate his new faith to a wider audience but dogmatic about the limited supply of his canonical texts. But from *Modern Tragedy* onward, his work suggests a massive estrangement from high culture, so that Cambridge, which plays an important role in both waves of dramatic criticism, undergoes a marked transformation of role.

Where he produced his first books as a kind of scholar in exile, dispensing culture to the masses from which he had only recently emerged, he wrote *Modern Tragedy* and *Drama from Ibsen to Brecht* as a disenchanted don, estranged from the academic community that had just welcomed his return by appointing him to a fellowship. Once again Williams proved he could only function in opposition to the institutions around him. Having spent his early years with the WEA in championing high culture, he reinstalled himself at his alma mater only to distance himself from all it stood for. His Cambridge undergraduates, unlike his WEA pupils, must look to working-class institutions—trade unions, shop floor committees, public houses—for distinctive examples of a culture that he now defined as "the whole way of life" of a community rather than the recreational activities of a privileged elite.

It is in terms of this new definition of culture that Williams investigates the tragic experience in *Modern Tragedy*. To prove that "we come to tragedy by many roads" (*MT*, 13), his book significantly alters the framework in which its topic is viewed. This is why he organizes his material into four sections: a history of academic theories of tragedy that subverts the notion of a single tragic ideal; a meditation on the tragic fate of twentieth-century revolutions, together with a testimony of commitment to the continuing struggle by the oppressed of all nations; a generically subversive set of readings that aligns the naturalist dramatists discussed in earlier books with works like *Anna Karenina, Women in Love,* and *Doctor Zhivago;* and a practical demonstration of modern tragedy in the shape of Williams's own play "Koba," the tragic history of a modern revolutionary.

In each part of *Modern Tragedy*, Williams mounts a campaign to wrestle tragedy from the hands of its academic spokesmen and to restore it to personal, social, and political experience. As a result, tragedy becomes less an academic genre descending in a clear line from the Greeks to the moderns than an experience continually redefined according to human need. When the moderns cling to the notion that tragedy involves special isolation or privileged excellence, they reveal their essential alienation from the ordinary pattern of their own lives. "What seems to me most significant about the current isolation of death," Williams remarks, "is not what it has to say about tragedy or about dying, but what it is saying, through this, about loneliness and the loss of human connection, and about the consequent blindness of human destiny. It is, that is to say, a theoretical formulation of liberal tragedy, rather than any kind of universal principle" (*MT*, 58). For Williams, it is social forms, rather than natural depravity or original sin, that drive men to self-destruction. In *Drama from Ibsen to Eliot*, he presented the naturalist drama as an alienated product, its words inescapably at odds with its action. In *Modern Tragedy* and *Drama from Ibsen to Brecht*, alienation is once again his central theme, but this time he ties it to the social conditions that produce the pervasive modern sense of isolation and loss, the bitter gap between the recurrent hope of liberation and its recurrent transformation into oppression.

In other words, Williams's later dramatic criticism stretches old obsessions across a much wider canvas. In *Drama from Ibsen to Brecht* and the second part of *Modern Tragedy*, he reinterprets the dramatists studied in *Drama from Ibsen to Eliot* in terms of an increasingly tragic socialist humanism. Yet in the same books he also sweeps boldly outward, to a wider range of plays, to the novel, to history itself. And everywhere he looks he confronts the same long revolution at work, the slow, mute rebellion against modern alienation. When he returns to the dramatists he studied before, his changing attitudes promote corresponding differences in interpretation. The significant dimension that in *Drama from Ibsen to Eliot* he thought Chekhov and Pirandello had missed can no longer be credited to a failure of verbal convention. It derives, he now recognizes, from a hollow at the center of contemporary life, a structural failure in modern society. "What Chekhov is essentially expressing is a common condition. . . . What is being expressed is not a dealing between persons, or a series of self-definitions; it is a *common*, inadvertent mood—questioning, desiring, defeated."[8] The final speech of Pirandello's *Henry the Fourth* now becomes "a new kind of theatre: a use of the theatre to expose itself, and then in the double exposure to question any discoverable reality" (*DIB*, 184). Our lives are arranged, Williams argues, in ways that make tragedy inevitable, whether we are defiant and isolated like Ibsen's Brand or cowed and conforming like Miller's Willie Loman.

But in *Drama from Ibsen to Brecht* and in the main chapters of *Modern Tragedy*, Williams provides an escape from this impasse, an escape offered by the dramas of Brecht. "On to an alienated world, that had been dramatized mainly from the inside," he observes, "Brecht turned an alienated consciousness: meeting a negative with a negative; intransigent, detached, open" (*DIB*, 332). As the epithets suggest, Brecht's "structure of feeling" closely matches Williams's own.

> Once again, the question is not: "should we admire or despise Galileo?" Brecht is not asking this. He is asking what happens to consciousness when it is caught in the deadlock between individual and social morality. Galileo's submission can be rationalised and justified, at the individual level, as a way of gaining time to go on with his work. But the point this misses is what the work is for. If the purpose of science is that all men can learn to understand their world, Galileo's betrayal is fundamental. . . . . The final scene, in which the manuscript of the *Discorsi* crosses the border, looks like a romantic liberation, unless we see also that the boys playing round the coach are still talking of witches.

The *coexistence* of these facts is always the point. . . . The movement of the play is from the ironic acceptance of false consciousness—what you say to get by, in an imperfect world—to the point where false consciousness becomes false action and is not irony but tragedy. . . . Tragedy in some of its oldest senses is certainly rejected. There is nothing inevitable or ennobling about this kind of failure. It is a matter of human choice, and the choice is not once for all; it is a matter of continuing history. The major achievement of Brecht's mature work is this recovery of history as a dimension for tragedy. (*MT,* 200–202)

In passages like these Williams's prose exhibits an eloquence that far surpasses the clotted repetitions of *Drama from Ibsen to Eliot* and that by sheer force of rhetoric merges dramatic criticism into a larger social and cultural vision. By standing the naturalist theater on its head, Brecht carried off a victory as liberating as Marx's inversion of Hegel. Brecht's plays at once push the conflict between the individual and society to its limits and understand this conflict in a historical and self-conscious way. This is why, at the climax of *Galileo,* when he presents the gifted individual, rather than the society around him, as the betrayer, Brecht offers "a radically different way of seeing an experience that is normally negotiated by . . . older conventions" (*MT,* 200). By tracing modern alienation back to its origins in identifiable choices made by historical individuals, Brecht made freedom a human possibility.

Yet it would be premature to suggest that in *Modern Tragedy* and in *Drama from Ibsen to Brecht* Williams displays a total openness toward his material, for once again he organizes his discussions around an all-encompassing central theme. Indeed, his later dramatic criticism represents one of the most ambitious undertakings of thematic criticism, synthesizing almost one hundred and fifty years of literary history into a never-ending conflict between individual and society. "The deepest crisis in modern literature," he observes, "is the division of experience into social and personal categories" (*MT,* 121)—a division that the critic himself must reject emphatically. What Williams calls "the long revolution against human alienation" (*MT*, 82) becomes a revolution he himself must fight on several different fronts, knowing that the battle against alienation begets "its own new kinds of alienation, which it must struggle to understand and which it must overcome, if it is to remain revolutionary" (*MT*, 82).

So terrible a battle must obviously influence the specific interpretations the critic decides to advance. Where Brecht's Galileo ignores his society and selfishly presses on with his research, Williams tempers his readings to the social deadlock he describes in "Tragedy and Revolution," the most contentious chapter of *Modern Tragedy*. In a situation where liberating visions must necessarily originate "in the actual suffering of real men . . . and in all the consequences of this suffering: degeneration, brutalisation, fear, hatred, envy" (*MT*, 77), a literary critic can hardly content himself with updating Bradley. But if Williams's revised readings do humanity some service, it is not so certain they do the same for their chosen authors.

When he looks at *Waiting for Godot*, for instance, he finds a fixed contrast between Pozzo and Lucky on the one side and Vladimir and Estragon on the other. The former inhabit "a formal world . . . an orthodox social relationship," while the latter have "a different essential relationship: informal and outside society (this is the real vagrancy); at once loving, doubtful and resentful, wanting to break away yet still anxiously returning to each other; a voluntary relationship, but with binding natural ties" (*DIB*, 346–47). It is frequently said that alienation has two sides, identity crisis and social breakdown. Beckett's plays have frequently been related to the first, less frequently to the second. Williams, trying to show how the two sides interact, offers significant distortions of both. Pozzo and Lucky could only be said to enjoy "an orthodox relationship" at a time preceding the abolition of slavery, while Vladimir and Estragon exhibit jarring antagonisms that the phrase "binding natural ties" seems inadequate to confront.

Beckett's world remains less predictable and more destructive than the one Williams teases out. In fact, the nuanced, familial relationship he sees between Vladimir and Estragon moves them closer to the characters in his own novels and plays than to Beckett's savagely alienated cartoons. Readers of *Border Country* and *The Volunteers* will compare these familial doubts and resentments, these anxious returns to the same valued but anxious relationships, with the "structure of feeling" Williams explores between Matthew Prior and his father or between Lewis Redfern and the Welsh village of Pontyrhiw. The three-inch ivory of human desolation that forms Beckett's world has been sacrificed on the one side to Williams's own sense of the pattern of personal relationships and on the other side to the larger canvas of alienation he mounts as his grand contribution to cultural history.

In *Modern Tragedy* and *Drama from Ibsen to Brecht*, Williams aims to understand tragedy historically and politically, showing that the self-consciousness forced on us by the theater of Brecht and Beckett should also govern our responses to the historical dramas of Suez, Cuba, and Vietnam. The liberal notion of tragedy, he notes, rests on the idea of "an action and a suffering rooted in the nature of man, to which historical and ethical considerations are . . . hostile" (*MT*, 37). Unfortunately, in both books he asserts connections between literary and political experience he fails ultimately to prove. No independent testimonies verify the alienation that he presents as the central connection between modern literature and society. *Modern Tragedy*, for instance, presents no evidence to support his thesis of social breakdown apart from the literary works that he cites as examples. In the same way, he argues that modern tragic theory has coldly ignored common suffering without naming any of its major exponents. Since he accuses these theorists of crimes ranging from pedantry to inhumanity it would be helpful if he identified the main perpetrators. It is as if he lived with the evidence so long that he never felt the need to expose it to public attention.

At some points in both books, Williams combines the worst habits of *Scrutiny* and *New Left Review.* From *Scrutiny* he takes his simmering sense of grievance and his tone of impassioned opposition to the received organs of tradition. From *New Left Review* he takes his willingness to erect one system and demolish another without ever exposing either to the limiting conventions of evidence. These deficiencies check the ambitiousness of his writing, which tries to provide social history and dramatic criticism in one leap. Moreover, the grand scheme of global alienation he uses as the key to his interpretations raises a still more intractable difficulty. He criticizes the liberal view of tragedy on the grounds that what it offers "as a total meaning of tragedy is in fact a particular meaning, to be understood and valued historically" (*MT,* 61). Yet he himself finds this a hard lesson to learn, for his own discussion repeatedly drapes history in a global alienation that he eventually links to existence itself rather than to social and political conditions. In the "delusion, loss of identity, the reduction of personality to a role and of society to a collective impersonation" (*DIB,* 184) that he criticizes at several points in these books, he discerns not an estrangement suffered under particular social conditions but "a generalization to life at any time" (*DIB,* 183). His urge to group as many dramas as possible into a common "structure of feeling" results, paradoxically, in a body of work that freezes history into one endlessly reverberating alienated moment.

* * *

The same all-pervading sense of an alienation that envelops the air like a mist visits Williams's own dramas, stifling the liberating impulses of revolution, draining the life out of the characters, and reducing the plays to actionless debates that end where they began, in the plight of lives distorted "into a wrong pattern, a killing pattern."[9] These words describe the steady progression into brutality undertaken by Joseph, the Stalin-like hero of

"Koba," the play Williams appended to the first edition of *Modern Tragedy* (1966). Set in an undisclosed country during a "present" that uncannily resembles Russia during the revolution, "Koba" ("the man who cannot be mastered") traces the political discussions by which the tyrant tries to consolidate his power. Unfortunately, neither the insurrection that brings Joseph to power nor the power struggles that punctuate his career ever erupt into onstage action. The moment of liberation and the long process of repression both occur at only a verbal level, and since the language Williams uses is largely that of debate and analysis, the play as a whole becomes a deadening one to read.

Williams wrote the play in 1959, the same year he started to plan the final section of *The Long Revolution*, his critique of the sprawling, directionless proliferation of the communications media in contemporary Britain. "Koba" examines a very different social possibility, for it charts the course of a revolution that began in blood and must be sustained by more blood. Unfortunately, its stasis recalls *Waiting for Godot* more than *Danton's Death*. A play about revolution that scarcely contains a significant action, it focuses instead on the long drift from humanity that afflicts its hero, whose zeal for revolutionary "discipline" and "hardening" strips him of the humanity that provided his initial revolutionary impulse. By degrees, Williams's hero detaches himself from anything but "the Party" and his own version of "History," now fetishized into a court of appeal for a "killing pattern" of "ashes, blood, death, misery, hatred."[10]

Yet Williams lacks the theatrical means to communicate the horror and the violence of a revolution whose leadership has withdrawn from humanity. What in his revised edition of *Modern Tragedy* he calls the "pity and terror" of revolutionary action, "the perception of a radical disorder in which the humanity of some men is denied and by that fact the idea of humanity itself is denied" (*MT*, 77), never comes to dramatic life. Williams can neither recreate this terror convincingly in the minds of his characters nor display it in spectacle across a stage. In sum, he finds himself in the dilemma he identified in Chekhov, whose commitment to a representational method condemned him "to show people dining, to depict their conversation in minor commonplaces" (*DIE*, 130). In "Koba," Williams lacks the technical skills to communicate the alienating qualities of revolution without draining his work of imaginative life.

Unlike Williams's other plays, "Koba" was never actually produced. Both "A Letter from the Country" and "Public Inquiry" appeared on BBC television, in 1966 and 1967 respectively. "A Letter from the Country" clearly arises from Williams's disenchantment with the Wilson administration that came to power two years before. It examines the changing relationship between Alan Pritchard, a Welsh schoolteacher, and Walter Dix, the Labour member of parliament who appears on "Everyday Politics," a Schools Television series that Pritchard uses for his classes on current affairs. But Dix also happens to be Pritchard's personal hero, the man to whom he has written regularly for eleven years and whom he thinks embodies the spirit of public accountability in government.

As it happens, it is the teacher who learns the first lesson, as he watches Dix slide into the familiar type of career politician whose idealism surfaces only at moments of stress. On one such occasion—the incident on which the play turns—Dix is unwise enough to blurt out sensitive security information to an overseas journalist. Pritchard, whom Dix has invited to the embassy reception where the slip occurs, is listening closely. The information appears in banner headlines the following day, and Dix's career seems at an end. Luckily, Tom Payne, a Harold Wilson-like minister who exhibits more mastery of the media than of human rights, has no intention of letting Dix resign, and he manages to deal with two separate waves of scandal that follow on his indiscretion. To kill the initial newspaper reports Payne arranges to be "interviewed." "Not a formal interview, we don't want to start playing it up. But casually, in passing, at the airport." To kill Pritchard's revelations (after the government denials he wrote to the press confirming the journalist's story) Payne invokes his ultimate weapon against press freedom, "official secrets" the public must on no account discuss. As a professional politician Payne acknowledges only the "real language" of politics, "our own language,"[11] a language that allows him to arrange events and policies so that they maintain only a minimal purchase on reality.

But in fact each of the characters has a very different sense of reality. Where Payne sees images to be manipulated, Dix sees men to be managed. Pritchard may serve as Dix's "conscience," but his daily work involves "a shifting coalition of actual men," with whom he must be "slow and reasonable, not always speaking out." Neither way of life appeals to Pritchard's wife, who rejects both "killing and arguing" in favor of the "binding natural ties" of a traditional society. "Alan teaching in school, and me with my neighbours. People living real lives, in the farms and the market. People marrying and bringing up children, and all giving their strength to live with each other."[12]

Only at the end of the play does Pritchard's own reality become clear. Earlier he had invited his class to "pick out one story and we'll follow it through." Now, however, he has become aware of the unbridgeable gap between career politicians and the people they represent. Why then, his wife asks, does he pack the London papers in his school bag? "What for? Since there's nothing" she asks. "Because there's nothing," he replies. "And because there's everything else." His letter remained unpublished, he now realizes, because it violated the secret code that holds together both Labour and Conservative governments, both left-wing and right-wing newspapers. The political language he instilled in his pupils is a language they must now unlearn together. "It's better like this," he concludes. "I'm not depending on him, or on any of them. I can do it myself."[13] Communication, he finally realizes, is too important to be left to professional communicators. The future belongs to people like himself, who can turn moral inquiry into public debate—and then keep on debating, through the whole course of their lives, denying the temptation to turn politics into images on the one side or personal relations on the other.

If British institutions freeze into artifice at the top, then at the bottom they wear away through exhaustion. "Public Inquiry" takes the pulse of men ruined by another kind of public service, the service offered by Welsh railmen at a small local station. Like "A Letter from the Country," "Public Inquiry" is an inside narrative, burrowing beneath official silences and public statements to the shape of lives behind the headlines. In this play, Williams takes the course his own studies always recommended to dramatists and engages with the details of ordinary working-class lives. The play centers on an unofficial and highly contentious wage claim, a claim that results in a strike-related train crash that leaves two workers dead and another subject to disciplinary action. In between these two spectacular events, Williams builds up a powerful sense of the demoralizing, piecemeal attrition of lives chained to "public service. . . . the hardest there is."[14]

This detailed knowledge of railway conditions and of the fears and aspirations of railway workers may well draw on Williams's own family background, for his own father spent almost his whole working life as a signalman at a small Welsh station. And it is interesting, too, that the accident at the center of the play results from the same generational conflict to which Williams returns again and again in his novels. In the play, however, he lays less stress on conflict than on the alienation that young and old both share. For in "Public Inquiry," the railway workers in the village have all become walking ghosts, alive only insofar as they can imagine a nostalgic past or a utopian future. Arthur, the railway veteran killed in the accident, reminisces about steam drives past, while David, who is indirectly responsible for his death, looks to the signal box of the future to free him from the three-shift system that has ruined his family life. According to David, "only the old men are staying. Only the old men now, are the willing railwaymen. . . . To get young men back on the railways, and to keep them when you've got them, which is a damned sight harder, it's money, it's bound to be money."[15] Yet David's militancy relies on his father's willingness to shoulder burdens he ought to meet himself. In fact, the climactic accident occurs only because of his father's tiredness, a tiredness he describes in terms of the self-estrangement that comes over him on night duty. "You're outside the box, looking in, and you see this man there. This man in dark clothes, and you ask who he is, what his life amounts to."[16]

Even so, David himself remains the most critical victim of the alienation that afflicts the railway community, for the alienation his father feels as he sits alone in the signal box David projects onto the system itself. In fact, he no longer sees human beings as operating the railways. His vision draws stark oppositions between the oppressions of the present and the utopias of the future, the rewards and privileges doled out to railway politicians and the public inquiries that victimize the workers. David is a man harrowed by his anger. "There's no reasonable language to say what I know," he asserts. Ironically, he addresses his grievances to a system and in the process destroys a relative. This, however, is not how he himself formulates his problems. "It's not only to my father I have to learn to speak. It's to all that broke him, to that whole condition."[17]

Working on the same lines as Brecht in *Galileo* or *Mother Courage*, Williams's television plays mount an inquiry into the alienating consequences of public service. However, unlike Brecht, he holds out little hope that the rank and file can break the pattern of betrayal established by the system that dominates them. Whether he sets his plays in Stalinist Russia, in Westminster, or in a Welsh village, his subject is always an all-powerful alienation that uses men as raw material for its own dehumanizing ends. In "Koba," he watches men grow hard as their own revolution hardens into political power. In "A Letter from the Country," he explores the way men accustomed to prestige and privilege separate themselves from their constituents. And finally, in "Public Inquiry," he dramatizes the steady erosion of morale that afflicts men without power.

Williams's television dramas undoubtedly pack more punch than "Koba." Yet, arguably, he lacks some of the equipment of a successful playwright. He is more fond of words than of action and more fond of discussion than of argument. Whether he is writing a critical study or a popular play, he always comes equipped with an ideological ax, so that in "Koba," for instance, he examines the Russian revolution as a disappointed believer rather than as a skeptical historian or even as a disinterested student of social change. And perhaps most damaging of all, his faith in the human capacity to enforce—or even to imagine—radical social change suffers frequent failures of force. One such failure occurs in the afterword he appended to *Modern Tragedy* in 1979, where his faith that mass action can overcome an ever intensifying alienation seems to flicker and die. At this point, his sense of an overwhelming estrangement dominates his sensibility. A "sense of diversity, of authentic tragic variations, is still my main emphasis," he observes, except that

> there is now this difference, that there is what seems to me a much wider gap between the realized and demonstrated historical and cultural diversity and the now apparently blank page of the future. . . . For much longer than now seems reasonable or even possible, we have endured disorder, and entered the struggle against disorder, with very simple convictions of the kind of future order towards which this struggle was directed. This trap has now been sprung. (*MT,* 216)

Williams has apparently succumbed to the malaise that in the 1950s he attacked across a whole dramatic tradition. At this point he himself capitulates to the vacuity he excoriated in Chekhov and Pirandello, in which "nothing, or nothing much, can be said, while we sail on . . . towards disaster. But we can play doomed verbal games, or talk past each other, in the ephemeral negative groups which human society has become" (*MT*, 215–16). Departing from his more characteristic stance—immunity to the disease that devastates those around him—Williams here plays a more spectacular role, as grand sacrifice to the alienation he now confronts as an inescapable human fact.

III. CULTURE

WITH the inevitability of a theorem, "Public Inquiry" plots the mixture of institutional expediency and individual exhaustion that subdues the lives of its working-class characters. The play appeared in 1967, nearly a decade after *Culture and Society* (1958) had reached very different conclusions about the condition of contemporary Britain. If "Public Inquiry" contains some of Williams's deepest fears about postwar Britain, then *Culture and Society* collects some of his most cherished hopes. For in that book, probably his most famous, he served as the great peacemaker, reconciling his working-class experiences to his knowledge of a predominantly middle-class tradition of cultural criticism in the hope of deepening his readers' appreciations of their common lives. Three years later, in *The Long Revolution* (1961), he could still speak of the gradual expansion of political and educational opportunities that made a bloodless cultural revolution a beckoning possibility. Yet by 1967, as we have seen, he was no longer so sure. And certainly, by 1973, when *The Country and the City* appeared, he felt he had to document extensively the economic and political apparatus that made estrangement rather than steady cultural development the prototype for modern experience. As a dramatist and a dramatic critic he had always acknowledged this estrangement; for a brief period, his cultural criticism appeared to move in the opposite direction. But, in 1973, he found himself back where so many modern intellectual ladders start, in a market society that only intermittently supported the intellectual's meliorist hopes.

Williams's work in the field of cultural studies as historian, theorist, lexicographer, and polemicist represents his single most important contribution to postwar intellectual history, for the tension between his loyalties to his rural, working-class roots and his recognition of the needs of "an unprecedented mobile urban society" has produced a body of work, in Frank Kermode's words, "of quite radical importance."[1]

Williams's cultural criticism separates itself from others in the field in at least three crucial areas. First, as Maurice Cranston has pointed out, it "provides a *socialist* theory of culture" and in this way "fills a conspicuous gap in the literature of socialism." Second, unlike most sociological, political, or even liberal theories of culture, it merges academic inquiry with personal witness. As E. P. Thompson has emphasized, Williams interposes his own personality as a major part of the evidence. "Even a brief passage of his writing has something about it which demands attention— a sense of stubborn, unfashionable integrity. . . . His work, over the past ten years, carries an authority which commands the respect of his opponents; and the positions which he has occupied must be negotiated by critics and by historians, by educational theorists, by sociologists and by political theorists." This remark also bears on the third point of originality, the fact that Williams rarely shelters behind subject or party specializations, so that his work frequently displays what Thompson calls a "partial disengagement" from affiliations either political or academic. In Asa Briggs's words, his work is situated at a "crossroads where different specialisms meet." Unable to respect disciplinary boundaries, he has proved uniquely "concerned not only with making his own contribution" to cultural debate but also with "clarifying the terms of the debate for other people. He has a genuine and unique personal contribution, grounded in his own experience as well as in his reading."[2] Williams's strength as a cultural critic comes from this unique fusion of multi-disciplinary inquiry and personal testimony, a combination that grants him the hearing denied to more dogmatic radicals like David Craig or Louis Althusser. Neither of these writers can be dismissed as narrow or sectarian; but neither provides the experiential underpinning that has gained Williams the respect of a public that prefers living experience to theoretical expertise.

British readers, at least, have agreed on Williams's exemplary status as a twentieth-century cultural critic. Even so, his work in the genre has not gone unchallenged, particularly when commentators focus on his style. Admirers and detractors alike agree that his command of the language is surprisingly weak for a major critic. His severest reader, an anonymous reviewer in the *Times Literary Supplement*, responded to *The Long Revolution* in these terms. "What looks like a 'general' book of real significance is so largely written in utterly humourless textbook language. The word 'we' is so daunting and hortatory that a sleepy reader may at any moment expect to be told, 'We next take a test tube. . . . '" Even a sympathetic reader like Richard Hoggart has argued that at times "the rhetorical balance of the cadences, the rhythmic repetitive structure of the periods, the alternation of large general statement with biblically or classically simple metaphor, do produce a rather orotund quality." But Dwight Macdonald perhaps raised the most penetrating objections when he said that Williams's style inhabited the pulpit rather than the resolutely secular, endlessly mobile world his prose described. "Mr. Williams' style puts the maximum distance between the reader and the subject. . . . The style is an end itself, a magical device for charming away . . . the threatening reality."[3]

In fact, the dispute about Williams's style provides access to an unresolved contradiction in his thinking. For if "experience" provides the surest measure of a culture's quality, if the critic himself repeatedly insists on the deep, organic connections between his proletarian origins and his work as a Cambridge don and radical intellectual, then why does his language so rarely communicate the fluidity and synthesis that his own life represents? Why does disjunction rather than conjunction provide his central trope? The answer, of course, is that his style registers his larger ambivalence about the nature and the purpose of culture. Is culture a privilege or a birthright? Does it embody "the best that is known and felt" or a whole way of life? Is it an evaluative concept or an anthropological tool? In the course of *Culture and Society, The Long Revolution,* and *The Country and the City,* Williams provides no consistent answers to these questions but takes rather what he calls a "democratic" approach to the definition of culture, underlining at every opportunity his sense of the diversity of cultural experiences and needs.

Put less sympathetically, this means that his style sometimes reflects a desire to reconcile all parties and to offend none. For instance, in his conclusion to *Culture and Society* he notes:

> There are still major material barriers to democracy, but there is also this barrier in our minds, behind which, with an assumption of virtue, we seek to lay hands on others, and, from our own constructions, determine their course. Against this the idea of culture is necessary, as an idea of the tending of *natural* growth. To know, even in part, any group of living processes, is to see and wonder at their extraordinary variety and complexity. To know, even in part, the life of man, is to see and wonder at its extraordinary multiplicity, its great fertility of value.[4]

His sentiments could hardly be more worthy or his expression more vague. Williams wants to transfer to the idea of culture as a whole way of life capital accumulated by a quite different idea, the Arnoldian idea of culture as "the best that is known and felt." For this reason, he borrows from the Arnoldian school its governing metaphor, the movement of a living organism that guarantees to culture the respect that human beings extend to natural processes. Unfortunately, his prose invokes such processes without properly defining their mode of operation. By speaking of "mental barriers to democracy," Williams reifies the human agents—entrepreneurs and demagogues—and the human characteristics—greed, snobbery, and selfishness—that impede democracy. His almost ritualistic incantation of "the life of man" fades into the same abstraction. Is man's "extraordinary variety and complexity" the first response of a visitor to a Calcutta

43

slum or a Ford production line? When Williams comes to formulate his cultural goals he forgets about "experience" and substitutes abstractions. The abstractions have the desired effect of reconciling opposing factions, but only because they fail to identify them precisely.

* * *

To understand why Williams produced his most searching and respected work in so evasive and abstracted a style, we must look once again at his own circumstances and, in particular, at his troubled association with the University of Cambridge after the war. When he returned to Cambridge to finish his degree and to undertake postgraduate work, Williams renewed his friendship with two fellow students, Wolf Mankowitz and Clifford Collins. The three decided to begin a journal that had the ambitious aim of uniting "radical left politics with Leavisite literary criticism" (*PL*, 65). Success in this goal would in effect reverse the course of English cultural criticism, which since the appearance of F. R. Leavis's *Mass Civilization and Minority Culture* (1930), Q. D. Leavis's *Fiction and the Reading Public* (1932), and T. S. Eliot's *The Idea of a Christian Society* (1939) had presented the modern world as the furthest point of a decline that began with the industrial revolution.

By 1947, Williams and his team had collected enough material to launch two journals, *Politics and Letters* and *The Critic*. A varied list of contributors included left-wing activists like Jean-Paul Sartre, G. D. H. Cole, and Christopher Hill; Leavisites like H. A. Mason and R. O. C. Winkler; and radical journalists like Wolf Mankowitz and George Orwell. In an ambitious editorial, "For Continuity in Change," Williams and his colleagues focused on what they saw as a growing cultural schism:

> There exists, it would be widely agreed, a dichotomy between politics and letters; between, that is, the direct tackling of the objective and impersonal problems of our society, and that

realization of the deepest levels of personality which is tradi-tionally associated with literature and the arts. In our genera-tion this problem has been stated at every possible level, and with the aid of every possible subterfuge. Its most familiar statement expresses a belief in the incompatibility of planned government with individual freedom. But too often, in this context, the affirmation of human values has served as noth-ing more than a protective screen to industrial and economic irresponsibility. . . . Opposition to evolutionary social change . . . has for us no secure foothold in moral argument, unless the most permanent and profound qualities of human experience (as seen, for example, in the writings of Yeats and Lawrence) are acutely known and personally known.[5]

To heal that schism, the editors proposed a fourfold pro-gram: to measure the mass uplift promised by postwar social planners against the traditional values of a high culture grounded on individual achievement; to increase their readers' understanding of the literary, social, and in-tellectual background of their own contemporary world; to apply the methods of a newly perfected practical criti-cism to a wider range of cultural forms; and to explore the relationship between society and literature in a more open-minded fashion than F. R. Leavis, whose essay "So-ciology and Literature" published in *Scrutiny* in 1945 ad-mitted sociology into criticism only insofar as it confirmed his prejudices about "the conditions of a vig-orous and spiritually vital culture."[6]

Williams and his colleagues promised to move be-yond the conservative view of *culture* as the leisured priv-ilege of a superior elite by incorporating into their own uses of the term references to the new town planning and public works programs, and to the proliferating appa-ratus of a postwar welfare state. They proposed to apply the methods of criticism introduced by Richards, Leavis, and Empson to the social forms of cinema, theater, broad-casting, and journalism. Following the road taken by L. C. Knights's *Drama and Society in the Age of Jonson* (1937) (a work Williams read repeatedly during these years), they undertook to explore the impact of the new social institutions on personal relationships and on literary forms. Contemporary literature could only be understood inside its social context, while the human implications of postwar social forms must also be spelled out. In sum, the editors promised to integrate modern literature into society, so "connecting private meaning with public fact, of making meaning responsible for fact."[7]

Despite an impressive list of contributors and a provocative statement of principles, neither journal lasted. *The Critic* appeared only twice, while *Politics and Letters* ceased publication in 1948. In retrospect one can see that neither succeeded in presenting an alternative critical position. It was one thing to outline principles distinct from the Leavisites, another to practice criticism in an entirely different mode. Winkler's essay on "Critic and Leviathan" (1947) took a familiar position when it deplored the incapacity of politics to emulate the complex subtlety of literature; but unfortunately his political quietism jarred with the abrasive, adversarial tone of his examinations of contemporary letters. Williams's own contributions borrowed some of F. R. Leavis's most browbeating tactics, plowing into Cyril Connolly and Noel Coward with the energy Leavis reserved for Lord David Cecil and Alfred Noyes. When Williams chose to inspect popular or continental culture he denounced it with a passionate intensity indistinguishable from *Scrutiny.* The devastating attacks he mounted on Dame Rebecca West and J. B. Priestley suggest that the journal's promise to report on popular authors amounted to little more than a readiness to judge them by the inappropriate standards of the metaphysical poets.

In the same way, the occasional novelty of Williams's material—his review of Salvador Dali's novel *Hidden Faces* or his discussion of modern Soviet socialist society—collapsed beneath his resolutely highbrow position. Dali, for instance, suffered the mandatory comparison with D. H. Lawrence. Where Lawrence's presentation of sexuality drew "a pattern from experience that is made up, in detail, of consistent discrimination as to value between elements of substantial living," Dali's "does not even treat of *experience*, but of behaviour," and so "demonstrates a corrupt consciousness, a superficiality of attitude and limitation of perception, which make his novel, in the last analysis, a waste of the reader's time."[8] On one page the critic reduced Dali to another example of mass sensationalism; on another page he decided that Soviet culture lacked the "third realm" a literary elite supplied in England. In short, Williams and his fellow editors ventured into the postwar world with the prejudices of prewar intellectuals. A new cultural politics could hardly be constructed from materials such as these.

During his last years as a student and his early years with the Workers' Educational Association, Williams frequently employed a style of literary criticism he had intellectually repudiated. It is significant that in *Reading and Criticism* (1950), an introductory work for adult education students, his analysis of Conrad's *Heart of Darkness* burrows into the verbal organization of the text without ever considering its colonial context. At this stage, Williams proved unable to write his own version of *Drama and Society in the Age of Jonson*. Instead, he worked as an almost microscopically close reader, unable to move away from verbal details despite his intellectual commitment to broader issues.

Fortunately, the materials for the synthesis between literary and social forms he needed to construct arrived unexpectedly from an entirely different quarter. In 1950, F. W. Bateson published *English Poetry: A Critical Introduction*. A year later, Bateson launched *Essays in Criticism* from Oxford, and Williams, currently serving as that university's WEA delegate, joined the staff as an assistant editor. Bateson concentrated on literary history rather than on the contemporary scene, but otherwise his aims matched those of *Politics and Letters* surprisingly well. In particular, he attacked critics who attended exclusively to verbal organization, suggesting that they would perform better if they understood the expectations of the writers' original audiences. Instead of rushing into those unremitting evaluations, critics should document the work's origins and reception. "Modern criticism has lost the sense of literary context. No doubt the actual words on the page are read as closely as ever before, but all that lies behind the words and the word-order—the forces, conventions and precedents that have made and modified them—is too often taken for granted. . . . [A] poem is not good or bad in itself but only in terms of the contexts in which it originated."[9] Bateson's remarks had implications beyond critical method. As Williams realized, they could provide a valuable instrument for the rapprochement between sociology and literature for which he had pressed so long.

By 1953, Williams had found his topic and a way out of the impasse that marked the end of *Politics and Letters*. Appropriately, considering his liking for verbal complexity, his liberation came by means of a word. In that year he contributed an essay entitled "The Idea of Culture" to *Essays in Criticism*. The essay maintained the attentiveness to verbal detail he exhibited in his earlier work, while adding a stronger sense of context and usage. When he unpacked the word *culture* he found three layers of meaning. From a relatively neutral reference to "the intellectual side of civilization," *culture* came to stand for "an ideal state of mind." But the usage that interested him most of all appeared in sociology and social anthropology, where *culture* denoted nothing less than "a whole way of life."[10] By situating the idea at the crossroads of all these meanings, Williams discovered a historical area of investigation, a way of understanding new social developments, and a method of intellectual inquiry—all at one stroke. What is more, the progress of *culture* from governing norm to subject area to method of inquiry in itself took in a whole field of social history. Williams's earlier attempts to integrate politics and letters foundered on the tendency for each realm to insist on its own dominance. The idea of *culture* provided a point d'appui, not least because a series of independent disciplines had made it central to their thought.

His discovery of the idea of *culture* in effect provided

Williams with a life's work. Between 1954 and 1958, he conducted a modest rehearsal for the complex cultural lexicography of *Culture and Society, The Long Revolution,* and *Keywords* (a book significantly subtitled *A Vocabulary of Culture and Society*) by compiling "A Natural History of Analogies" in the pages of the WEA journal *Highway.* In a series of modestly proportioned contributions of a thousand words each, he examined some educational *idées reçues*: *ladder* as applied to educational opportunity, *standards* as applied to classroom assessment, *class* and *classes* as applied to social divisions.[11] These short pieces allowed him to track shibboleths back to their sources and to identify the particular social interests and cultural biases they served. It was at this point that he began to subordinate the interests and methods of Cambridge criticism to his own unique form of cultural history. Instead of analyzing words according to fixed Leavisian criteria like "particularity" or "concreteness," he now adopted the more flexible practice of Bateson, who referred any ambiguities to the endlessly complex interaction of much larger forces.

* * *

The more substantial results of these inquiries into the relationship between language and social change appeared in *Culture and Society* (1958) and in *The Long Revolution* (1961). In *Culture and Society,* Williams identifies five key words—*industry, democracy, class, art,* and *culture*—that had acquired significant dimensions of meaning during the first years of the industrial revolution. "There is in fact a general pattern of change in these words," he argues, "and this can be used as a special kind of map by which it is possible to look again at those wider changes in life and thought to which the changes in language evidently refer" (*CS*, xi).

Why has this particular work amassed and sustained such an exceptional reputation in literary and cultural studies? Clearly, the words with which Williams begins provide only starting points for a larger inquiry that strides across literary criticism, social history, politics, and sociology in its attempt to repossess a previously unconnected strand of British social thinking and to validate it for contemporary conditions. On its publication in 1958, *Culture and Society* represented by far Williams's most ambitious work to date, principally because of his determination to proceed on so many different fronts.

In the first place, he compiles a comprehensive account of British cultural criticism that unifies its many mansions in one distinctive lodging. The principle of contrast around which he organizes his opening chapter, juxtaposing conservative Edmund Burke against radical William Cobbett, nostalgic Robert Southey against utopian Robert Owen, becomes the shaping principle for the whole book. Williams brings into a single framework the ideas of radical activists (E. P. Thompson, George Bernard Shaw), utilitarians (John Stuart Mill), pugnacious conservatives (T. E. Hulme, D. H. Lawrence), humanitarian socialists (R. H. Tawney, William Morris), aesthetes withdrawn and engagé (Walter Pater, John Ruskin), and the whole procession of intellectual withdrawal from modern industrial society that stretches from disgruntled artisans like George Gissing to Olympian clerics like T. S. Eliot.

In the second place, Williams refuses to set his sources at each others' throats or to inject his own opinions into the debates he presents. If his last chapter implicitly challenges his twentieth-century authorities by setting down his own notes toward the construction of a common culture, still the body of *Culture and Society* betrays none of the compulsive desire to evaluate by a single measure of excellence that marred *Drama from Ibsen to Eliot*. In maturing as a critic, Williams had mellowed as a writer, so that he could present heterogeneous evidence without harrying it into a small stockyard of radical cliché.

In fact, behind the word *culture*, which he initially encountered as a battle cry for a disgruntled elite, Williams uncovers a much deeper seam of social criticism. The book's third contribution lies in the way his detailed history of the idea of culture from 1780 to 1950 feeds a complex, considered discussion of contemporary society. Are modern audiences no more than masses, passive consumers of commodities fashioned by entrepreneurs, as Dwight Macdonald and others contend? Williams deconstructs the idea of the mass audience by presenting it as a treason promulgated by intellectuals since the very birth of industrial society. Is the affluence enjoyed by increasing numbers of the working and middle classes sufficient in itself to produce a just society? Williams assembles testimonies from Ruskin, Morris, and Gissing all calling for a quality of life the market alone could never provide. In this context the verdict of J. K. Galbraith's *The Affluent Society* (1958), published the same year as Williams's book, that the modern redistribution of wealth disguised public squalor as private affluence, gained substantial historical support. Modern society illustrated the diffusion of economic wealth without social justice demolished in R. H. Tawney's *The Acquisitive Society* (1921), while Tawney's diagnoses seemed even more alarming when understood in terms of the long intellectual alienation from modern society that *Culture and Society* for the first time uncovered.

The book's fourth, and possibly most decisive, contribution lies in its demonstration of the importance of the organic metaphor in British cultural thought. Just as M. H. Abrams's *The Mirror and the Lamp* (1953) presented organicism as the revolutionary principle distinguishing romantic from neoclassical aesthetics, so Williams shows the same metaphor underpinning the radical cultural tradition that *Culture and Society* (1958) almost simultaneously unfurled. Moreover, by amassing a variety of authorities who saw culture as a process penetrating every aspect of public and private life, Williams fashioned a weapon against a whole spectrum of contemporary groups, from the new multinational industrialists, to the managerial socialists of the British Labour left (a group as dedicated to the production of commodities as the capitalists themselves), to the consensus sociology of Talcott Parsons, which reduced modern society to a predictable network of normative expectations.

In fact, without *Culture and Society* the work of the British "new left," with its sustained critique of British social and political institutions, might never have occurred. In a move of great audacity, Williams recaptures tradition, a territory Eliot used to declare war on the present, and makes it the means of access to an egalitarian future. Eliot's tradition reached back to Dante to nourish the individual talent. Williams's reaches back to Southey and Burke to increase awareness of the common culture. By viewing culture as both an individual vision and a communal reality, Williams returns cultural criticism to its origins in Coleridge and the romantic poets. In this way his book tracks a direct path between the idealist testimonies at its start and his own proposals for working-class uplift set down in his groundbreaking final chapter. As a result, *Culture and Society* becomes at once an act of repossession, an act of reconstruction, and a genuine act of creation.

Yet Williams's most influential book is not necessarily his most optimistic. Although he speaks rather mildly of the "wider changes" in thought from which his inquiry begins, a powerful sense of estrangement sustains his history of the idea of culture from Edmund Burke's high ideal at the beginning of the industrial revolution to its bankrupt state in the inhumane, alienated society of George Orwell's *1984*. Indeed, the force that Burke invested with almost supernatural qualities at the start of the book has withered to the betrayed, bitter consciousness of Winston Smith by its end, and Williams's faith has withered alongside it.

As he was perhaps the first to point out, the idea of *culture* as an organic, natural, traditional way of life appeared only in the wake of a revolution that destroyed forever its living remains. This, presumably, is why he later described *Culture and Society* as "an oppositional work," one that repudiated a long line of British culture critics by exposing the contradictions from which they worked. "I knew perfectly well who I was writing against," he observed in 1977. "Eliot, Leavis and the whole of the cultural conservatism that had formed around them—the people who had pre-empted the culture and literature of this country" (*PL,* 98, 112).

Yet it is difficult to square Williams's later account of his aims with the experience of reading his book. Even in his guarded conclusion he admits that "the tradition it records is a major contribution to our common understanding," as well as "a major incentive to its necessary extensions" (*CS,* 338). In other words, his assessment of the propaganda for culture offered by writers like Coleridge, Matthew Arnold, D. H. Lawrence, and F. R. Leavis proceeds in the best traditions of liberal sympathy. Also liberal in tone is his emphasis on succession rather than on schism. Certainly, his wide-ranging survey of the definitions of culture offered by British writers establishes very convincingly the continuity of the tradition he uncovers. For the idea of *culture* as a settled way of life connects writers as far apart as Edmund Burke and D. H. Lawrence, T. S. Eliot and F. R. Leavis. Burke and Lawrence both sponsor a primitivism that sets the traditional, settled ways of *culture* against the disturbing claims of an industrialized society, while Eliot and Leavis come together under one roof as champions of the organic society, even though a chasm separates Eliot's Christian commonwealth from Leavis's exclusively literary domain. The tradition of *culture* as Williams presents it yokes opposites together and cements the strangest of alliances.

But perhaps the strangest alliance involves the critic himself, who adopts another article of faith from the tradition he dissects when he makes "experience" a value irrespective of its social referent. Newman's idea of culture, Williams reports, rested "on a convinced experience of the divine order" (*CS,* 127). Romantic authors discovered in art "a mode of human experience and activity which the progress of society seemed increasingly to deny" (*CS,* 39). The sum of these "experiences," he agrees, is a tradition that offers the best understanding to date of the schis-

53

matic tendencies of postromantic culture. Having begun his book by showing how the modern idea of *culture* originated in an industrial revolution that denied it any real existence, he allows his accumulated evidence to transform *culture* into an unquestionable value identified with nothing less than "experience" itself.

By describing *culture* as an "experience" that is intrinsically valuable, Williams effectively closes his inquiry before it gets under way, for to understand the idea more deeply would have taken him into the crises of political and economic history that provoked British intellectuals to adopt it as a slogan. Occasionally, as in his discussion of Matthew Arnold, he does include this kind of archival material. More often, however, the idea of *culture* spurs him, like a long line of thinkers before him, to desert the world of men for the ethereal realm of ideas. In Burke, "what survives is an experience, a particular kind of learning; the writing is important only to the extent that it communicates this. It is, finally, a personal experience become a landmark" (*CS*, 5). Burke might never have espoused a cause or proselytized for a faction from the way Williams describes him. Similarly, Carlyle embodied in his view of culture "the governing seriousness of a living effort, against which every cynicism, every kind of half-belief, every satisfaction in indifference, may be seen and placed, in an ultimate human contrast" (*CS*, 86). Williams's Carlyle is neither a working man of letters nor an uncompromising polemicist: he has been transported to a realm where he sleeps with kings and councillors far away from the social crises that provoked his sponsorship of *culture* as Williams understands it.

Moreover, by referring so many of his instances to an "experience" that seals off social and historical investigation, Williams deprives himself of any instrument to understand the very different status *culture* enjoys in its progress from the nineteenth to the twentieth century. This, in turn, limits his understanding of the modern developments that have sustained the idea. One immediate consequence is that he falls in with some powerfully distorting currents set in motion by his own contemporaries. In many fields, from poetry to social history, modern thinkers have conceived of their century as in search of a tradition that will restore it to unity. The works of Eliot, Ransom, Tate, and Richards provide powerful—but very different—accounts of a schismatic modernity that becomes whole only by recourse to panaceas like "mythology" and "the image." Williams himself promised to take a different approach, using language itself as a gateway into larger social forces. In the end, however, his concentration on language lands him in the narrowest trap of all. For after D. H. Lawrence *culture* occupies a progressively smaller realm. T. S. Eliot uses the idea as a *cordon sanitaire* to exclude Jews, to confine the working classes to their country of origin, and to boost the case against social mobility, while I. A. Richards and F. R. Leavis entrust to a literary minority the roles and responsibilities Coleridge allotted to a whole social class. Increasingly, the cause of culture is heard only in the voices of "sensitive, kindly, lonely men" (*CS,* 181) like Shaw and Gissing, who use the word to disguise their alienation from an increasingly mechanized and powerful public world. The hope that *culture* could mean an enlargement of the common life withers in the face of cases such as these.

Because he shares the Leavisite preference for particulars rather than for larger movements, Williams presents his book not as "a series of abstracted problems" but as "a series of statements by individuals" (*CS,* xvii). But this arrangement makes impossible the kind of historical investigation he originally promised, since the key words from which he starts never return to the social occasions that called them forth. This weakness also undermines his more programmatic concluding chapter, where he argues that the experiences embodied in working-class culture would make a valuable addition to the record he has compiled. In these pages, he no longer contents himself with recording a tradition but acts as spokesman for progressive social change by arguing the case for a "common culture" that would heal the divisions caused by *class* and *industry*. A working-class culture sustained by community solidarity could, he argues, blend harmoniously with a middle-class culture that presents individualism and service as its chief ideals.

The symmetrical structure of this "common culture," with its appealing combination of middle-class achievement and working-class solidarity, conceals important weaknesses in its composition. In narrowing working-class experience to the organized activities of trade unions and labor organizations, Williams idealizes a way of life that has not proved the summum bonum for many. As well as organizing themselves to improve their lots, the working classes have endured their fair share of violence, debt, illiteracy, failed relationships, job dismissals, unemployment, and conflicts with the law. As Frank Kermode, another prominent British working-class critic has pointed out, working-class society is more characterized by "its promiscuous social contacts and neglect of privacy" than by its fine sense of integrity and order.[12] Williams fashions his idea of working-class life in the image of Arnold's high culture, so that it stands for the best and most informed experiences the working classes have to offer rather than for working-class experience as a whole. "When we speak . . . of a working-class idea, we do not mean that all working people possess it, or even approve of it. We mean, rather, that this is the essential idea embodied in the organizations and institutions which that class creates: the working-class movement as a tendency, rather than all working-class people as individuals" (*CS*, 326). Unfortunately, few working-class people inhabit the kind of small rural community Williams himself knows best, where "the essential idea" of working-class life appears considerably more clearly than in a sprawling metropolitan estate or high-rise. Nor, of course, did that community prove vital enough to accommodate its spokesman, who probably abstracted from it a way of life that had changed by the time he adopted it as an ideal or that perhaps never existed at all in the way he remembers it.

56

Finally, by tagging a discussion of working-class culture onto a discussion of an entirely different tradition, Williams fails to examine in any depth the two very different ideas of culture that have sustained intellectual and working-class lives. For the writers examined in the main part of *Culture and Society,* the word *culture* stood for a value, a court of appeal, or a personal inspiration. But in his last chapter Williams uses the idea in an anthropological sense, to stand for the network of customs and institutions that constitute the way of life of a particular social class, without noticing that these two meanings stand at either side of the great divide that has separated intellectuals from the larger life of society since the last years of the eighteenth century. His proposals for a common culture proceed as if the alienating consequences of that period had no force, as if it took only good intentions to realign intellectuals, exploiters, and masses in a richly diverse and harmonious common life.

* * *

In *The Long Revolution* (1961), Williams tries to remedy these deficiencies by laying stronger theoretical and empirical foundations for his revitalized "common culture." In particular, he takes issue with what he considers a persistent fallacy in contemporary thinking on these matters, the notion that politics, economics, and culture function as autonomous and separate realms. Such thinking, he argues, leads to the "dominative" mode that characterizes modern society, in which each realm pursues its own perfection without considering the social process as a whole. He cannot accept this recurring separation, which he traces back to an initial division of men into masters and servants. Such divisions dominate our ways of seeing, living, and relating to the world. They sever our actions into work and leisure, consuming and creating. They sort our children into a gifted few and a commonplace many. They concentrate political decisions into a centralized power base manipulated by an estranged minority. Periodically, these perceptual and social divisions erupt into disturbances—strikes, walkouts, wage disputes—that betray the alienating mechanisms of a market-based society disguising itself as ordinary living. Williams does not doubt that modernity is unprecedentedly estranging. "Our contemporary experience of work, love, thought, art, learning, decision and play is more fragmented than in any other recorded kind of society." Moreover, he insists that these divisions run against our stubborn, ineradicable need to shape experience into more abundant and creative wholes. "Yet still, necessarily, we try to make connexions, to achieve integrity, and to gain control, and in part we succeed" (*LR*, 136).

Like *Culture and Society, The Long Revolution* returns obsessively to the social and personal alienation of industrialized Britain, a society that Williams elects as his area of study on the grounds that he knows it best and that, in any case, the British experience stands for modernity as a whole. But unlike the earlier book, *The Long Revolution* moves obliquely along three separate fronts. In the first part of his study, Williams mounts a complex argument to show that "the creative element in man is the root both of his personality and his society" (*LR*, 134). In the second part he provides a documentary survey of the institutions—education, the press, authorship, the public libraries—that have governed British cultural life since the nineteenth century. His last part, a speculative and probing report on "Britain in the 1960s," complements the long concluding chapter of *Culture and Society*. In both books he proposes a common culture that will lead the country out of its current divisions and dislocations into a vital and organic caring society.

In the first part of *The Long Revolution*, Williams makes a polemical attack on some potent contemporary assumptions about the relationship between self and society. Creativity, he argues, is the prerogative not of the artist but of all men. The mass market and the cult of the isolated artist are two sides of a coin that devalues the creative potential of the average individual, who is too often

58

regarded as economic raw material or one among many of the "philistine masses." How effectively do existing institutions nourish this creativity into growth? In a valuable second part, Williams provides a documentary record of such organized manifestations of culture as the media, publishing houses, the secondary schools, and the universities. Some of this work would be extended in his *Communications* (1962) and in *Television: Technology and Cultural Form* (1974). In this section, the weight of his evidence restores to cultural analysis a social and political history it customarily lacks. He provides, for instance, a description of the social backgrounds of English authors that gives documentary proof of the dominance of Oxford and Cambridge in English literary life, a dominance not previously verified by external sources. He then exposes the falsity of a common educational assumption by showing that the ideal of a "liberal education" has only governed British life for a relatively short time. It would be more accurate, he notes, to see medieval education as vocational, even though its subject matter formed the basis of a gentleman's "classical" education in later periods. When he turns to the media he notes that a "popular press" spawned by the masses and shunned by a discerning minority did not appear hard on the heels of the 1870 Education Act. According to circulation surveys, the tabloid is as popular with the wealthy as with the poor. By taking a long perspective, Williams can make significantly fresh judgments about the transmission and consumption of cultural forms.

Even so, the theoretical speculations of part one and the documentary evidence of part two remain ancillary to the hope he expresses in part three "of creating a new kind of social consciousness" (*LR*, 357). At a time when many individuals relate to society as consumers, vagrants, exiles, or rebels—as anything but members—such a consciousness becomes indispensable, and Williams will not leave the task of creating it to the media or to politicians. In these pages, his frustration with a Labour party unable to conceive of change as anything other than "modernization" becomes readily apparent, while his antipathy to a Conservative party that he sees as the tool "of the propertied and the controllers" (*LR*, 353) derives from class and regional attitudes he at no point tries to subdue.

Throughout his book, Williams offers a wealth of testimony to the institutions and behaviors that separate human beings from one another. Schools consolidate the stratification begun at birth rather than stimulate creative potential. At work, the demands of the market organize labor into units that promote "efficiency" by reducing workers to instruments of production. At play, these same workers become units of consumption. At periodic intervals, these automatons elect representatives who streamline the political process according to the same market laws. How, then, is it possible to undercut this institutional compulsion to diminish human diversity into mass uniformity? Williams's proposals falter at this point. He argues that "the 'massification' of society can only happen . . . if a majority of the people . . . accept this version of themselves. . . . While no significant version of other people is there as an alternative, the degrading version makes easy headway" (*LR*, 378). Yet one need look no further than his own earlier works to see alternative possibilities. Was not *Culture and Society* an anthology of alternatives to "massification"? If life in 1961 is as alienated as life a hundred years before, then the lack of imagined alternatives to mass society can hardly provide the excuse, for cultural history could fill an imaginary museum with such possibilities.

Williams implies that genuine social and institutional change would occur if individuals extended to the social process as a whole the kind of complex, considered expectations they gave to their own lives. Although the attitude "I'm all right, Jack," enjoys a popularity in Britain "as an interpretation of our majority social feelings," in fact "very few people . . . would accept this attitude as an adequate description of their *own* feelings" (*LR*, 379). At the end of the line as Williams presents it, everyman becomes his own John Ruskin engaged in a "long revolution" that could will a common culture into being through consciousness alone. Unfortunately, a society's controlling institutions are unlikely to fall into common hands without either a quantum leap in the average consciousness or a seizure of power by an increasingly apathetic majority. The proposals Williams makes for internal adjustments to existing social arrangements—more regular elections, mass access to television and the press—do not seem sufficient to conquer so deep seated a malaise.

In *The Long Revolution* Williams presents two aims that seem both separately and mutually inconsistent. First, he wants to make a gradual transition toward a radical change in consciousness, a hope that drives him back to the Labour party whose slow parliamentary reformism he had earlier condemned. And second, he wants to saturate culture as a whole way of life with the creative potential he criticizes "high culture" for adopting as its own, a scheme that tacitly recognizes a social ladder he claims to have outgrown. It is inconsistent too that the ambitious program developed in the third part of his book implicitly narrows "experience," an idea that in *Culture and Society* stood for a range of inherited, social, and personal evaluations, down to the free play of individual consciousness. In fact, the Williams of *The Long Revolution* and the Matthew Arnold of *Essays in Criticism* have much in common. The drastic changes they both envisage in the common life would need to set the liberating potential of consciousness to work in the civil and economic realms. Neither critic is prepared to believe that access to these might call for a very different kind of revolution.

IV. SOCIALISM

W ILLIAMS completed *The Long Revolution* in 1959. These were difficult times for the left in western democracies, which saw the millennial impulses of radical socialism absorbed in a general drift toward affluence and accommodation. In important ways, his works of this period found themselves conditioned by contemporary expectations. *Culture and Society* assembles a record of radical protest against industrial society but dissociates itself from the hostile tone and uncompromising condemnations employed by many writers in a tradition that stretches from Ruskin's *Fors Clavigera* to Eliot's *After Strange Gods*. Williams wants to integrate working-class experience into this tradition, but only selectively, in its more orderly and institutionalized aspects. The same desire to iron out potential conflict propels *The Long Revolution*, where the record of inequality and middle-class dominance he sketches in British educational and cultural institutions will permit conclusions more radical than the gradual, cautious measures he allows himself to propose. In the last pages of that book Williams approached the very limits of a consciousness that could be accommodated to existing social and political institutions. The cautiousness of his criticisms of British society—his long, pondered passages on whether *bourgeois* retains any useful meaning in the mid-twentieth century, for instance— belongs to the period of Daniel Bell's *The End of Ideology* (1960) and Anthony Crosland's *The Future of Socialism* (1956), a period less fascinated by ideology than by consensus.

But by 1965, when he began to write *The Country and the City,* the materials for a very different kind of history lay at hand. In 1963, E. P. Thompson's *The Making of the English Working Class* appeared, providing a documentary record of radical proletarian protest and middle-class reaction that drastically modified the gradual, progressive view of British social history of Williams's earlier books. The next years yielded an increasing supply of raw material for a history written from a distinctively working-class perspective. Emmanuel Le Roy Ladurie's thesis *The Peasants of Languedoc* (1966) recorded the history of an obscure French village. Michel Foucault's *Folie et déraison* (1961) explored the underside of the age of reason by writing a history of institutions for the insane, while Christopher Hill's *The World Turned Upside Down* (1972) offered a version of the seventeenth century made not in the image of T. S. Eliot's lost world of orthodox civility but as a subversive, millenarian counterculture.

Williams's own politics moved steadily leftward during this period. In 1965, he signaled the beginnings of his more active engagement with international movements by joining the University of Cambridge's Vietnam solidarity campaign. Two years later, alongside two fellow leftists, E. P. Thompson and Stuart Hall, he began to draft the *May-Day Manifesto 1968,* a document that unequivocally rejected the technocratic, managerial vision of the Labour party. His work on the editorial committee of *New Left Review* from 1959 to 1972 took him even further away from the cautious quietism of *Culture and Society,* renewing his contacts with a more radical form of socialism.

Williams has always obsessively returned to his own writings, reworking them according to shifting ideological currents or his own personal obsessions. In *The Country and the City,* he undertakes to rewrite *Culture and Society* by viewing the machinery of capitalism from the perspective of those displaced by it, the exploited and unlettered with whom he now overtly identifies. In *Culture and Society,* he muffled his own voice in order to trace a complex line of predominantly middle-class protest against industrialization, while relegating his working-class experience to his conclusion, where it became one element among many in the construction of a common culture. From the very first pages of *The Country and the City,* his own experience as a Welsh socialist commuting to a Cambridge whose social and ideological function he deplores determines the course of his argument. *The Country and the City* represents his response to the critics who saw *Culture and Society* as too neutral, too abstract, too eager to defuse political conflicts in a Britain where affluence and consensus politics papered over a history of imperialism, class struggle, and state repression.

It is no surprise, then, that what Max Byrd called "a new tone of impatient, personal anger" burst into *The Country and the City* in 1973.[1] In *The Long Revolution*, Williams's evidence of the divisive qualities of cultural institutions seemed more compelling than his proposals for integration. No such weakness impedes the progress of *The Country and the City*, which provides a continuous history of exclusion and oppression. For the first time, Williams refuses to accommodate his social responses to a dominant picture of culture or order. Instead, like Foucault, he tries to restore a neglected group to social and literary history. Like Foucault too, he writes an adversarial history, reading in the authorized versions of the past just so many specious justifications for the brute fact of power.

One of Williams's most ambitious works, *The Country and the City* has five main goals. First, he attacks the false nostalgia that has pervaded accounts of British rural life since the eighteenth century. Second, he offers what he calls the "real history" of the countryside by exposing the economic considerations that have dominated social relationships there. Third, he counters official social history by providing his own short studies of some individuals neglected in the usual "capitalist" histories. Fourth, he presses his campaign on a literary front, penetrating the conventions of rural and urban literature to expose the social relationships they mask. But all these goals are ultimately subsidiary to his fifth and most ambitious argument, that urban capitalism merely intensified and reorganized a system of exploitation originating in the country.

Williams wants to redress the received mythologies

about urban socialism and rural conservatism, an ambition that gives a new, abrasive edge to his writing, which now crackles with the urgency of a prophet. The quasi-scriptural tone Richard Hoggart noted in *Culture and Society* now becomes harnessed to the voice of an embittered Elijah. This, for instance, is how Williams describes capitalism in its feudal dress:

> From inside and outside there was this remorseless moving-in of the armed gangs, with their titles of importance, their kingships and their baronies, to feed from other men's harvests. And the armed gangs became social and natural orders, blessed by their gods and their churches, with at the bottom of the pyramid, over a tale of centuries, the working cultivator, the human and natural man—sometimes finding a living space, a settled working area; as often deprived of it—but in any case breaking the land and himself to support this rising social estate, which can be seen to culminate in the medieval "order" of the Norman and then the English kings: a more complete because more organised and more extended exploitation, under its banner "Feed him ye must." (*CC*, 38)

Williams's style has frequently been criticized for its inability to come to grips with concrete particulars. *The Country and the City* marks a shift in presentation as well as in ideology, as this passage indicates. Where he once packed his paragraphs with abstractions, he now mans them with hostile forces. His account of feudalism has an epic sweep in keeping with the violence and the force that sustains the epic vision. Against the imposed hierarchies with their pyramid of privilege and esteem he pits the subsistence living of the uncelebrated laborer, "breaking the land and himself" in support of a system that exploits him economically and ignores him culturally. "There is only one real question," he continues indignantly: "Where do we stand, with whom do we identify?" (*CC*, 38)

But clearly, Williams marshals his opposing forces so that the reader can return only one answer to this question. He no longer writes to inform or even to persuade;

his abiding purpose now is to convert, to enforce our commitment to his own version of social and cultural history. Yet can any "real history" proceed by such ruthless divisions into predators and victims? Before we make a commitment, we should surely know more about the object of our commitment than that he embodies "the human and natural man." If Williams wishes to realign his readers from the Rousseau of *The Social Contract* to the Rousseau of *The Confessions*, he should make this more clear. As the passage stands, it asks us to make historical judgments without presenting anything more than materials for moral disapproval. Where official history proceeds by naming the powerful and viewing the ordinary as an anonymous mass, in the manner of Shakespeare's *Henry V*, which asks "Where is the number of our English dead?" and then numbers them as

Edward the Duke of York, the Earl of Suffolk,
Sir Richard Ketly, Davy Gam, esquire;
None else of name,

Williams promises to reverse this procedure but only succeeds in making his victims as anonymous as his predators. At this point his prose has become more colorful—but scarcely more concrete.

Williams's revisionary purposes extend to his literary interpretations. In Greek pastoral, he acknowledges a genre able to accommodate the realities of country life as a whole, as a working cycle of plenty and scarcity, exhaustion and replenishment, loss and renewal. But in the degenerate form of Renaissance pastoral he finds only the daydreams of a privileged class. Where Greek pastoral embraced a whole social order, Renaissance pastoral masks social realities in a world of artifice and play that presents the countryside as just another source of conspicuous consumption. The literary foreshortening comes after a more drastic foreshortening in reality that destroyed the settlements of the many to stock the artificial needs of the few. It is in this way, Williams argues, that poetic conventions come to serve as stage properties for a dominant class, which uses them simultaneously to mask and to justify its social control. From now on, exclusion will provide a recurring motif in the development of the pastoral genre, whether in the Jane Austen who moves across a landscape reduced to real estate, making "settlements, alone, against all the odds, like some supernatural lawyer" (*CC,* 116) or in the George Eliot who denies to her agricultural laborers the intense moral scrutiny she lavishes on her middle-class protagonists.

In *The Country and the City,* Williams offers tantalizing connections between literary pastoral and real social history. Even so, the single-minded conviction he brings to his discussion of a notoriously ambiguous genre frequently does it rough justice. Sidney's *Arcadia* becomes an "elegant game" (*CC,* 22); the Sidney family are allowed to participate as expropriators while their other achievements go unacknowledged. Wherever Williams moves he finds evidence of "the explicit forms of the long class-society" (*CC,* 106), an image that now replaces the gradualist organicism of his earlier books. "The corporation country-house, the industrial seat, the ruling-class school" (*CC,* 106): these are what he cannot help but remember when he reads even the most remotely pastoralist work.

As he admits right from the start, his responses to literary pastoral smart with the impact of his own separation from a Wales never able to support its population, a problem that deeply changed the lives of both his father, who worked on the railways, and his grandfather, a roadman. His father, Williams recalls,

had been as much born to the land as his own father, yet, like him, he could not live by it. That man, Joseph, my grandfather, was a farmworker until middle age, when he lost his job and with it his cottage, and became a roadman: cutting and clearing along a length of the road that led away to the Midlands, to other cities. . . . We were a dispersed family, along the road, the railway, and now letters and print. These were the altering communications, the altering connections, between country and city, and between all the intermediate

> places and communities, the intermediate or temporary jobs and settlements. (*CC*, 4)

Williams wants to knit his personal narrative of dispossession into a larger pattern of expropriation he sees as reaching down to a present in which "the dominant mode of production and social relationships teaches, impresses, offers to make normal and even rigid, modes of detached, separated, external perception and action: modes of using and consuming rather than accepting and enjoying people and things" (*CC*, 298). Behind the tautological insistence of the style lies Williams's overwhelming conviction of the alienation he must expose in contemporary social forms. Where "experience" in *Culture and Society* provided a universal currency, rich enough to accommodate Burke and D. H. Lawrence, it now stands for something monolithic and estranging. *The Country and the City* pitches its net wide, but its principle of selection always turns on the same initial act of expropriation Williams now sees as dividing humanity into the predators and the dispossessed. Any cultural document that takes no account of this division he accuses of "insolent indifference to most people's needs" (*CC*, 84).

Yet, arguably, Williams's own position becomes as culturally and imaginatively impoverishing as the acts of appropriation he condemns. How else can one explain his reference to the "ordinary literary-historical version" (*CC*, 84) of country life, a formula that presumably yokes royalist Spenser to puritan Milton, countryman Wordsworth to Georgian Edward Thomas? Williams lumps together poems, journals, and novels in order to decide whether they constitute a "true history" without considering speakers, situations, or modes. He accumulates conventions—of country house poetry, of pastoral, of narrative fiction—without discussing in any realistic way what needs the conventions were designed to meet or what artistic purposes they were constructed to serve. Since he professes to see only two purposes behind conventions—they either expose a "true history" or they con-

68

ceal it—he effectively collapses the distinction between fact and fiction, art and history. In his own aesthetics, just as much as in the aesthetics he repudiates, art exists only as the instrument of more powerful purposes. The result is a criticism that not only reduces the diversity of artistic conventions but also abolishes the independence of art. Where literature does not imitate a "real process" (*CC*, 82), it deceives with its "enamelled world" (*CC*, 18). The necessity for both, in a life that necessarily contains diverse experiences, is something that Williams seems unwilling to concede in this book.

Worst of all, his narrative often suffers from a sentimentality that fails the very class whose cause it aims to serve. If Williams drastically reduces the realm of art, he also shields his own version of social history from any more astringent version of reality. Alexander Somerville, author of *The Autobiography of a Working Man* (1848), is one of the excluded whose history Williams wants to restore to public view. And his narrative is certainly an extraordinary one:

> After years of labouring and poaching he took the shilling as a soldier, to escape unemployment, and after he had enlisted he wrote a letter to a newspaper saying that the troops would not turn out against a demonstration in support of the Reform Bill. He was discovered and viciously flogged. He became a hero in radical circles but continued to drift and eventually became an informer. *Whistler at the Plough* was written in the agency of the Anti-Corn Law-League. Later he emigrated to Canada. (*CC*, 189)

Williams thinks Somerville's career "reminds us of the ambiguity of some of the articulate observers of working rural life" (*CC*, 189). But he does not seem happy with this ambiguity, since he goes on to assert that "Somerville's one wholly independent expression of opinion was savagely punished" (*CC*, 189). But by the same yardstick, did Somerville not succumb to a certain viciousness in becoming an informer? Williams reserves all his indignation for the upper-class oppressors and shuffles awkwardly about any conduct less than utterly noble in its victims. He confines his instances of absolute depravity to one class, which means that he inverts history without reconstructing it.

Joseph Arch, another of Williams's Victorian working-class heroes, enjoyed a brief period as a rural activist. As a young man he founded a farm workers' union; as an old man he became a member of parliament. In Williams's eyes, this history resolves itself into a simple pattern of youthful commitment and elderly accommodation. "Much of his early spirit was in the end patronised and incorporated, as happened similarly with most of the urban labourers' representatives" (CC, 191). Williams offers his nugget histories of working-class saints in the spirit of *The Golden Legend*, so that their every action becomes comprehensible in terms of some grand plan of expropriation. This admittedly makes for compelling reading. But as social history it lumps all its material into the grand scheme of alienation his last pages triumphantly unfurl.

Williams cannot acknowledge changes in political affiliation or simple personal drift as authentic experiences, since they reduce the monolithic authority of his alternative history. Yet it remains arguable whether his final explanation belongs to history at all, since it gathers the whole of human experience into a grand expropriating plan. His central division between country and city helps us to understand, he suggests, a whole spectrum of divisions that

are the critical culmination of the division and specialisation of labour which, though it did not begin with capitalism, was developed under it to an extraordinary and transforming degree. Other forms of the same fundamental division are the separation between mental and manual labour, between administration and operation, between politics and social life. The symptoms of this division can be found at every point in what is now our common life: in the idea and practice of social classes; in conventional definitions of work and of education;

70

in the physical distribution of settlements; and in temporal organisation of the day, the week, the year, the lifetime. (*CC*, 304–5)

Williams again invokes his epic machinery to organize the flux of history. In fact, this passage alerts us to the whole structural principle of *The Country and the City*. Throughout the book, he habitually moves from the dramatic local instance—Somerville's flogging, the expulsion of his own grandfather from his cottage—to the larger historical process, the devouring machinery of a capitalism that grinds its victims into standard units in a larger, but equally formless, whole. This habitual movement often seduces by its rhetoric, and, piece by piece, it grows into a moving autobiographical testimony of Williams's disenchantment with British culture. But as an instrument for understanding that culture, it makes the book as a whole a considerably less useful document than *Culture and Society* and *The Long Revolution*, since its main authority comes from the critic's own highly developed sense of estrangement. Behind his initial division into country and city Williams sees a whole chain of exclusions and subordinations. At this point it makes no sense to him to speak of mass culture, of minority culture, or even of the death of culture. The common cultural experience, he concludes, is of alienation—his own alienation endlessly rewritten. By the end of *The Country and the City*, he can see only a long train of divisions intellectuals themselves have helped to drive. From here he could move in only one direction, toward the ambivalent and ultimately hostile encounter with contemporary Marxist theory that would provide the starting point, more or less explicit, for his next four critical books.

* * *

The general trend in non-Marxist criticism—Patrick Parrinder's valuable article of 1984, "The Accents of Raymond Williams," is a case in point[2]—is to see a falling off between the like-minded Williams of *Culture and Society* and the abstract, theoretical, and militantly revolutionary author of *Marxism and Literature*. Marxists themselves, not surprisingly, have thought exactly the reverse. For instance, in *The Function of Criticism*, also published in 1984, Terry Eagleton describes Williams's work under the rubric "historicist humanism," noting that over its vast range there are "patches . . . which suffer from insufficient technical knowledge and a lack of rigorous theorization."[3] Williams himself has been in two minds on this question. On the one hand, he has frequently emphasized the continuity in his thinking, for instance by republishing in his *Problems in Materialism and Culture* (1980) work from the 1950s through to the late 1970s. On the other hand, in *Politics and Letters* (1979), he expressed reservations about what is possibly still his most influential book, *Culture and Society*, while two years later he anticipated Eagleton's critique by writing a short study called *Culture* (1981) in a considerably more technical vein.

The late 1970s and the 1980s signal Williams's outright departure from the conventions, assumptions, and procedures of British empirical criticism. In these years he prefers to cite Goldmann, Lukács, and Timpanaro rather than Coleridge, Eliot, and Leavis. Even so, he moves among the Marxist intellectuals only to upset some of their traditional theoretical wares. In *Marxism and Literature* (1977), he conducts an intense, obscure, internal debate with Marxist views of language, literature, and culture. In *Problems in Materialism and Culture* (1980) and *Writing in Society* (1983), two volumes that collect lectures and papers delivered over a nearly thirty-year period, and in *Culture* (1981), he offers accessible, even popularizing, discussions of some of the most recondite issues in Marxist theory—the relation between base and superstructure, the status of ideology, the processes of social and cultural reproduction. Often he resorts to the lecturer's ploy of addressing a received thesis—that an economic base determines the activities of a cultural superstructure, that culture operates separately from material processes—by tracing the circumstances in which it emerged or by disputing its own key words.

At each point, he painstakingly dismantles the fallacies he encounters, patiently demonstrating how previous thinkers have reinforced our sense of an ineradicable alienation between man, society, and nature. In his four most overtly theoretical books, Williams always seems at odds with some reigning orthodoxy among the intelligentsia, whether it be Althusser's version of Marxism, Lévi-Strauss's structuralism, McLuhan's technological determinism, or formalism as promoted in Russia and Cambridge. As an alternative to these approaches, he makes out the case for a new discipline: "the analysis of all forms of signification, including quite centrally writing, within the actual means and conditions of their production" (*WS*, 210). In a world of electronic media and computerized information, "society" becomes a problem in communication at the very moment when traditional literary culture loses its communicative force. In a push button age, literature and society alike must be reexamined from a perspective that Williams calls "cultural materialism" (*ML*, 5). In the 1970s and the 1980s, he argues, the central problem of Marxist theory becomes not so much the ownership of the means of production as the ownership of the means of communication. In other words, his engagement with Marxism follows a highly selective path, one that follows the pattern of his earlier interests in culture and communication in order to show how these potentially alienating forces interact with human beings in the changed conditions of a postindustrial society.

* * *

The first of these self-consciously theoretical books, *Marxism and Literature* (1977), offers clear evidence of Williams's dissatisfaction with British literary criticism on the one side and with orthodox Soviet Marxism on the other. Unhappy with an account of the artwork that elevates it to

73

magical status or relegates it to secondary product, he looks to "the later work of Lukács, the later work of Sartre, the developing work of Goldmann and of Althusser, the variable and developing syntheses of Marxism and some forms of structuralism," as well as to the Frankfurt School and the Marx of Grundrisse for assistance (*ML*, 4). Williams works elements from this material into "an argument based on what I have learned from all that previous work, set into a new and conscious relation with Marxism" (*ML*, 6).

Not surprisingly—since he has only just over two hundred pages at his disposal—his book reviews and revises some of the commonplaces of Marxist theory with forbidding compression, allowing, for instance, five pages to the sociology of culture and six pages to genre. The effect is something like a haiku version of Proust's *Remembrance of Things Past*. Of twenty-four chapters in the book, only two—those dealing with "Language" and "Ideology"—have more than fifteen pages, and only two more—those dealing with "Culture" and "Literature"— run to nine pages. The remainder, which includes "Conventions," "Genres," "From Reflection to Mediation," "The Sociology of Culture," and, more bewilderingly, "Aesthetic and Other Situations," range from five to eight pages in length. In his chapter on "Authors," Williams refrains from mentioning any authors other than God or Christ, or from citing any authorities other than Marx, Goldmann, and Lukács, guiding his reader into the discussion with the almost sibylline remark, "To see individuation as a social process is to set limits to the isolation but also perhaps to the autonomy of the individual author. To see form as formative has a similar effect" (*ML*, 192). Whatever else Williams intends, he ensures that his conversion, like St Paul's, will not be understood too quickly.

Like the convert, he signals his estrangement from the British critical establishment by a tortuous linguistic compression. By the same token, however, his alliance with Marxism remains an equivocal one. He makes little attempt to open sustained discussion with the Marxist thinkers he lists as influences, spends much time revising Marxist categories, and retains much of his private vocabulary. Readers who hoped to see the phrase "structure of feeling" replaced by something less resoundingly undefined would certainly be disappointed. In effect, the book offers a retrospect of topics that have interested Williams in the past and a prospectus for work he would conduct in the future. The work itself viewed independently remains too drastically abbreviated to be comprehensible.

Problems in Materialism and Culture (1980), a collection of essays that extends over a twenty-year period, allows Williams to explore at length some of the problems merely sketched out in *Marxism and Literature*. The collection evidences his dissent from liberal cultural criticism and orthodox Marxism alike, opening with a polemical rebuttal of Matthew Arnold and closing with a call for a revisionary socialism that would take account of the historical shift from a society organized around the construction of material products to a society organized around the control and dissemination of knowledge. Repeatedly, Williams revises socialist commonplaces in the interests of complexity. Repeatedly, he attempts to lessen the priority of economic matters in Marxist theory in order to update it for application to an "information society." Too often, he argues, Marxist analysis has reinforced the alienated categories of capitalist thought. In his careful discussion of "Ideas of Nature," he suggests that Marxist sloganizing about "conquest" and "colonialization" owes too much to capitalist categories to prove useful to a radically different assessment of human capacities. In pursuit of this assessment, Williams sometimes seems to want to shock Marxist thinkers out of complacency by a sort of Wildean audacity, as when he notes that the formula of economic base and cultural superstructure is "essentially a bourgeois formula."[4]

Problems in Materialism and Culture demonstrates Williams's skill as a debater, a public figure willing to address and to revitalize key Marxist issues. In comparison, *Culture* (1981) becomes a more disappointing volume, resembling a syllabus with its topic headings and briefly worked examples. The book apparently has the classroom in view, as Williams traces the subject area and methods of what he calls a "sociology of culture." His eight short chapters study the institutions and groups that have historically produced culture; the material means—books, paintings, electronic media—by which culture has been disseminated; the various modes in which cultural products are recognized; the history and sociology of specific cultural forms such as Greek tragedy and English Renaissance drama; the theory of cultural reproduction; and the institutions, from medieval crafts to modern corporations, that control this reproduction. Williams dutifully cites sources and dates—Altick, Weber, Barthes, Gombrich, Marx, Macherey, Goldmann, Gramsci—but the "field" the book sketches out amounts to little more than a set of separate disciplines (sociology, cultural history, social anthropology, literary criticism). Without the twin commitment to personal and social rediscovery that characterized Williams's earlier work, the very idea of *culture* loses some of its interpretative force.

Williams tries to remedy this loss in the last of these theoretical collections, *Writing in Society* (1983). Like *Problems in Materialism and Culture*, the book measures the duration and intensity of Williams's long dissent from what he calls "English" culture. Its earliest offering, written in the year of the Suez crisis and the Hungarian revolution, shows Williams as a poet, upbraiding in verse the contributors to the influential *New Lines* anthology that launched Larkin and the Movement in 1956. Williams attacks the poets for their low-key "end of ideology" political stance, their understated idioms, and their suburban range of reference. The last group of essays, written between 1981 and 1983, reinforces this long record of dissent by launching a many-angled attack on the organization of the English syllabus at Williams's own university. In fact, his chosen title, *Writing in Society,* in itself challenges two key assumptions of Cambridge English: the belief in the primacy of the literary; and the assumption that literature can be studied in isolation from other forms of human thought.

Williams objects above all to the institutional separation of literary and language study. It results, he argues, in a radical estrangement of the "literary," which becomes a fetishized object, the vehicle for national nostalgia and political reaction. In three papers—"Cambridge English, Past and Present," "Crisis in English Studies," and "Beyond Cambridge English"—he traces the steady dwindling of "literature" from reference to all printed matter, to fictional creation, and finally to the narrow range of canonical texts Cambridge sanctions as "tradition." As soon as "literature" in this radically diminished form became the norm it took on elitist, chauvinistic, and sectarian qualities. Transmitted to a social elite by a self-conscious cultural minority, it rehearsed minority sensibilities in an ever-dwindling body of material. In its least harmful form, Cambridge English produced the myth of cultural decline promulgated by *Scrutiny*. In its most noxious form, it became an orthodoxy imposed by an "assertion of order through a version of tradition" (*WS*, 220). At one side lay the apocryphal organic society of George Sturt's *The Wheelwright's Shop*. At the other lay the blatantly authoritarian order of Eliot's *After Strange Gods*.

Williams tries to reverse such assumptions by presenting literature alongside other cultural creations, so that the tradition of elect witnesses compiled in *Culture and Society* becomes the record of multiple testimonies—Welshmen like Jack Jones and T. Rowland Hughes, women writers like Charlotte Smith and Mary Wollstonecraft, marginal writers like Robert Tressell and Ursula K. Le Guin—recorded in *Writing in Society*. The shift in title is significant, for the Williams of the late 1970s and the 1980s sees writing not as a privileged accompaniment to social change but as a mode of communication within a larger social system. From a tradition of "culture and society" erected by a selection of exceptional witnesses, he hopes to create a discipline of "culture in society" that would fuse sociological, formal, and technological inquiries into something more humanly powerful than its component parts. On the one side, "cultural materialism" would give questions of cultural production and transmission a more central role in Marxist thought. On the other side, it would overcome the liberal alienation between culture and society by viewing culture itself as a central social process.

Cambridge English devoted itself to the preservation of a "culture" it viewed as national, timeless, and the possession of a minority. When Williams turned to Marxist cultural analysis, however, he recognized rivaling inadequacies. In the classic Soviet Marxism of Engels and Plekhanov he saw an unwillingness to grant the constitutive power of culture or to concede its radical part in every aspect of human activity. In the British Marxism of the 1930s and the 1940s he attacked in some of the most astringent pages of *Culture and Society,* he noticed an antithetical range of obsessions, a willingness to ransom Marxist economic theory to an essentially romantic view of culture. The British socialist tradition reflected in Alick West's *Crisis and Criticism* (1937), Ralph Fox's *The Novel and the People* (1937), and Christopher Caudwell's successive *Studies in a Dying Culture* (1938, 1949) remained fixed in an idealism that could not engage with the social existence of cultural movements without beating a periodic retreat into the alienated individual consciousness.

Such was the nature of the Marxism Williams condemned in *Culture and Society.* By turns hopelessly idealistic and flagrantly materialistic, this tradition had little to teach him. He encountered another problem in the swelling adversary culture of the late 1960s, which produced major reorientations in social theory that threatened to destroy the whole basis of his previous work. His own theory of culture rested on a traditional anthropology that identified specific cultural practices as expressions of a larger way of life. But for the theorists who became prominent in the 1970s, culture became a language, an abstract system of oppositions and exclusions. A program like his own, pinning its hopes for social and cultural change on organized labor and on education, now bore the brunt of radical attack. Moreover, the very existence of a working class at the vanguard of revolutionary change, or even progressive reform, could no longer be guaranteed by a society whose economy provided services rather than products. How would Williams, habitually worried by his alienation from his working-class roots, confront the possible disappearance of the working class?

In a sense, contemporary Marxists had decreed an end not just to the historical individual situated in a particular social class but to the whole idea of experience and history as potentially liberating forces. In the structuralist Marxism of the 1970s and the 1980s, Williams noted a rejection of consciousness and tradition as agents of radical social change. The idea of structuralism as developed by Lévi-Strauss and applied to Marxism by Louis Althusser presented culture in terms of a "system" or an "apparatus" structured like a language that maintained a class dominance by inserting itself into the perceptual and conceptual processes of both the exploited and the dominant groups. Althusser's bold binary oppositions—on one side "science," the ground of rigorous theoretical practice and the instrument of real discovery; on the other side "ideology," reproducing the inequalities of the existing social system[5]—could not have pleased Williams, who had always grounded his radicalism in the possibilities for liberty the estranged consciousness could entertain and the institutions it could establish to make those possibilities real. Williams's radicalism had always fueled his humanism, a humanism that now fell into the trashcan of a history itself under grave attack. For instead of history, a polite disseminator of ruling-class fictions, Michel Foucault preferred to speak of "genealogy," an instrument for deconstructing the dominant ideological system. "Man is an invention of recent date," he triumphantly announced, "and one perhaps nearing its end."[6] Refracted through lenses like these, culture and human freedom appeared miles apart.

Similar distortions emerged when Marxist theorists looked more narrowly at literature itself. Where Soviet Marxism marginalized culture, following a "first bread, then circuses" scheme of human development, European Marxists acknowledged its claims with an almost Brahminical exclusiveness. Georg Lukács, for instance, saw modern literature as "the adoption of perversity and idiocy as types of the *condition humaine*." Instead of "the dialectic between man-as-individual and man-as-social being" of classical realism, contemporary writers presented man as "by nature solitary, asocial, unable to enter into relationships with other human beings."[7] Modern art was the product of the long isolation from society that left writers from Kafka and Joyce to Beckett and Henry Miller sweltering in a wasteland of fractured personalities and disintegrating relationships. Only the great tradition of Balzac, Tolstoy, and Mann (and the conventions of Soviet realism) sustained the critic in this unpromising climate.

As a result, Lukács's tradition became even more drastically curtailed than Leavis's: his canon could find no room for Beckett, Faulkner, Joyce or Musil; and his powerful example encouraged a series of rival condemnations by younger critics. For Althusser, no less than for Lukács or Leavis, art embodied a value that could not be conferred indiscriminately. Like Lukács, whose "realism" included Balzac and Mann, but rejected Zola and Beckett, Althusser insisted that by "art" he meant "authentic art, not works of an average or mediocre level."[8]

But clearly, European Marxists could not even agree among themselves about the status of modern art, for they answered the schismatic crisis of modern culture by erecting dogmas and founding sects of their own. Where Lukács attacked modernist obscurity, Walter Benjamin found modernity too philistine to meet his esoteric needs. In his view, the modern world threatened the authenticity of classical art by substituting "a plurality of copies for a unique existence." Where Baudelaire and Proust had an "aura" that reinforced an older cult of the artist as magus, the cinema turned art into a form of commodity capitalism and so lay the foundations for fascist rule. "The film responds to the shriveling of the aura with an artificial build-up of the 'personality' outside the studio. The cult of the movie star, fostered by the money of the film industry, preserves not the unique aura of the person but 'the spell of the personality,' the phony spell of a commodity."[9] In an age of mechanical reproduction, the masterpiece became an endangered species.

Marxist cultural analysis as undertaken in Lukács's *The Meaning of Contemporary Realism* and Benjamin's "The Work of Art in the Age of Mechanical Reproduction" could understand cultural change only in terms of catastrophic shifts in the social order. These writers proved incapable of understanding the continuing, non-epochal relationships between society and culture Williams himself wished to explore. Cultural criticism written in this mode shared *Scrutiny's* dogmatic conviction that the contemporary represented the shadow of the past without its substance. Lacking what Perry Anderson calls "the tension of a direct or active relationship to a proletarian audience,"[10] these powerful European thinkers took an increasingly mandarin attitude to the contemporary world. In Althusser, in Lukács, and in the Benjamin who fondly conceived of himself as the last man in Europe, Williams found only the fragments for an eschatology of culture, not the foundations for the sociology of culture he longed to write.

However, the Europeans supplied Williams with some more promising leads in the work of Lucien Goldmann and the Bakhtin circle. Unlike Althusser and Foucault, Goldmann saw consciousness as a necessary instrument for liberation. Unlike Benjamin and Lukács, Bakhtin saw language in terms of speech and literature as a constellation of ordinary social exchanges. Cultural change must, Goldmann insisted, be viewed in terms of "the psychic structure created and developed by organizational capitalism." But the organized media need not only serve a dominant class, and the mechanisms involved were not inevitably alienating. "Even if the path is very long and detours through a chain of devices and machines, at the end of the chain there is always a human being whose consciousness, we know, can in no way 'overlook' what is important." Goldmann, like Williams, pledged himself to "a strategy which would permit efficacious action by those trying to use mass media toward effectively creative, cultural ends."[11] Neither writer could assent to Benjamin's view that electronic communication paved the way for fascism.

Mikhail Bakhtin's writings also confirmed Williams's views on the social origins of language and literacy. From primal utterance to complex literary discourse, language presupposed a social act comprehensible only in social terms. But even the masterpiece did not necessitate language raised to a power only an elect could comprehend. In *Problems of Dostoevsky's Poetics* (1973), Bakhtin interpreted this novelist's complex, many-voiced oeuvre in terms of a single "polyphonic" whole, so that individual novels became the site for a string of competing discourses that stretched from the popular idioms of folktale, sentimental romance, melodrama, and fable to the sophisticated codes of the European realist tradition. Seen in this way, Dostoevsky came to inhabit Williams's own border country of private self-examination and public inquiry. "Every thought of Dostoevsky's heroes . . . senses itself to be from the very beginning a *rejoinder* in an unfinalized dialogue. Such thought is not impelled toward a well-rounded, finalized, systemically monologic whole. It lives a tense life on the borders of someone else's thought, someone else's consciousness."[12] For Bakhtin, the term *masterpiece* suggested not a sovereign object with its own aura but the confluence of a series of intersecting traditions. In Bakhtin as in Goldmann, Williams found theoretical vindication of a belief that had sustained his interrogations of the meaning and function of culture for over twenty years, a belief incapsulated in the title of one of his earliest essays: "Culture is Ordinary."[13]

In his theoretical collections of the 1970s and the 1980s, Williams tried to develop a position that would overcome his own divisions by acknowledging the importance of culture in ordinary experience. If the Cambridge critics reified *culture*, Marxists either ignored it or denied its liberating possibilities to the community as a whole. Whichever way Williams looked, the idea of culture as a social product, the result of common human activity and the expression of collective human needs, seemed alienated and estranged. To overcome this estrangement, he needed to alter the terms in which both *culture* and *society* were normally viewed. In *Culture,* he observes that the very idea of a social class may need adjustment if it is to prove useful in modern conditions. He reminds his readers that "a social class is by no means always culturally monolithic" and may accordingly "have alternative . . . cultural, often religious, affiliations which are not characteristic of the class as a whole."[14] He concedes to orthodox Marxism that a "dominant" culture exists to enforce ruling-class norms and prohibitions. But he points also to the existence of "residual" and "emergent" cultures that embody experiences and values beyond the dominant culture's range of expression (*C*, 204). He identifies a source for these values in the rational group of social actors he calls a "class fraction" (*C*, 74), a group within a class that dissents from certain class norms.

When Williams moves to concrete examples, the usefulness of his distinction becomes clear. For instance, working-class culture during the 1840s remained locked within middle-class norms, just as middle-class culture, despite its economic dominance, had difficulty breaking free of aristocratic motifs. One obvious example is the inheritance plot, which outlasted Fielding and even Jane Austen to become a dominant paradigm in working- and middle-class writing of the period. This is why, in "Forms of English Fiction in 1848" (*WS*, 1977), Williams insists on taking the widest cultural sample, unearthing in the process a mass of historical romances, adventure stories, working-class autobiographies, aristocratic sex scandals, and bourgeois apologias. And unlike orthodox Marxist analysts, he refuses to line up such materials according to their progressive or reactionary bias, for this, he argues, would miss the experience of struggle that characterizes cultural no less than economic history.

Rather than presenting cultural change as a see-saw of progressive and reactionary forces, Williams prefers to use his concept of the "class fraction" to explore a variety of relationships between class affiliation and cultural forms. To examine the Godwin circle is, he argues, to discover identifiable assumptions and values rather than the statistically quantifiable similarities appropriate to political or demographic analysis. When he turns to the Bloomsbury group, his concept of the fraction enables him to calibrate the exact measure of estrangement and compromise between its members and the ruling class. His concluding judgment, that for members of the group "the social conscience, in the end, is to protect the private consciousness" (*PMC*, 167), actually comes close to the judgment of F. R. Leavis's essays on "Keynes, Lawrence and Cambridge" and "Keynes, Spender and Currency Values" (*Scrutiny*, 1949, 1951) thirty years before. Yet the basis for the judgment differs greatly. Leavis and Williams both share an instinctual dislike for Bloomsbury, but where Leavis emphasizes the group's betrayal of a continuous tradition of moral criticism from Bunyan to *Scrutiny*, Williams enmeshes it in the contradictions of an unequal social order it wanted to see partially reformed. He does this by providing a substantial history of the ruling class from which the group intellectually dissented, showing how its intellectual aspirations clashed with its position at the apex of the colonial order.

Williams's "The Bloomsbury Fraction" (1978) provides the basis for a new way of writing Marxist intellectual history. In the same period, he attempts to make more complex the drastic process of canonization and excommunication that passes for Marxist literary history. In *Criticism and Ideology* (1976), Terry Eagleton announced that "the major fiction of Victorian society was the product of the petty bourgeoisie. The Brontës, Dickens, Eliot, Hardy: it is with them, rather than with Thackeray, Trol-

lope, Disraeli, Bulwer Lytton, that the finest achievements of nineteenth-century realism are to be found."
Within a page Eagleton could speak without qualification
of a "petty-bourgeois realist tradition" that, with just the
right spirit of enterprise, extends to Gissing, Wells, and
Bennett by the end of the century.[15] Williams is more cautious. Can "the stereotyped terms 'bourgeois fiction' and
'bourgeois realism' " be applied to *Jane Eyre* and *Wuthering
Heights,* he asks an Essex University audience eager for
reflections on the year of revolutions (*WS,* 152–53)? Surely
not, he replies, since "you are not asked, as in the ordinary account of bourgeois realistic fiction you are sup-
posed to be asked, to identify with a single point of view
on the experience. The opportunities for very complex
seeing, both within a given situation and within time
through a developing situation, are built into the form of
the novel" (*WS,* 158). Where Eagleton related the fractured
narrative perspective of *Dombey and Son* to Dickens's con-
fusions as a petty-bourgeois thinker, Williams acknowledges a "subjunctive mode," the presence "beyond the
terms of the realist text . . . of a quite different but attain-
able perspective" (*WS,* 161).

Williams maintains an almost completely adversarial
relationship with Marxist cultural criticism. He suggests
that its formulas fail to acknowledge the specificity and
diversity of ordinary experience, so that the term "bourgeois realism" will tell us as little about *Wuthering Heights*
as the term "working-class fiction" will tell us about
Robert Tressell's *The Ragged-Trousered Philanthropists.*
Marxist critics like to lump working-class experience into
one block, the easier to align it against a class enemy. In
his edition of *Hard Times,* David Craig includes Tressell
alongside Blake, Cobbett, Ruskin, Morris, Sillitoe, Engels, Marx, Kropotkin, and Dickens himself as an instance of "the classic line of labour analysis."[16] Williams's
analysis of Tressell's novel proceeds in a completely different direction, pointing to a book whose shifting discourse
and alliances across class lines open on a reality more
mixed and heterogeneous than orthodox discussion con-

cedes. As an independent socialist thinker, Williams shows some of the liking for the exceptional case of the unorthodox Marxist Walter Benjamin, who preferred Goethe to Schiller, Baudelaire to Hugo, and *trauerspiel* to high tragedy. Ironically, the indignant activist of *The Country and The City* (1973) turns, in the course of the decade, into a cautious, analytical thinker, a socialist more at home in the graduate school than on the picket lines.

Clearly, Williams's rapprochement with Marxism only partially overcame his deep-rooted sense of intellectual alienation. In *Marxism and Literature* (1977), he embraced a strand of revisionary Marxism that included the Frankfurt school, the Bakhtin circle, and the Marx of *Grundrisse.* Yet only two years later, when he reassessed his career from the same revolutionary socialist perspective in his self-searching and self-revealing *Politics and Letters* (1979), he formulated his commitments cautiously, even hesitantly, without any of the confidence in the socialist cause exhibited by his interviewers.

> So far as the shift from a reformist to a revolutionary perspective is concerned, I think that still if I saw an area in which the first kind of course seemed possible, I would always follow it until I was finally convinced that it was not just difficult, or interminable, or intractable, but that it was actually delaying the prospect of a solution. (*PL*, 410)

The labyrinthine syntax of this remark owes more to the author of *The Princess Casamassima* than to the author of *Capital.* Williams edges uncomfortably toward revolutionary socialism more from a sense of blockage in contemporary institutions than from a faith in an inevitably emancipating future. As John Sutherland remarked in a *New Statesman* review entitled "Problematical," Williams's work did not grow simpler as it moved leftward. Its inspiration remained his own dissociated sensibility, his own "complex self-definition and self-location," his own divided allegiances to his origins and to his intellectual life.[17]

* * *

If *Marxism and Literature, Culture, Problems in Materialism and Culture,* and *Writing in Society* offer considerable incidental revaluation of Marxist discourse, their more substantial claim to originality rests on the new field of study whose lineaments they sketch out. Williams's most significant achievement in these books and in the two studies of the media, *Communications* (originally published in 1962 but extensively revised in 1966 and 1976) and *Television: Technology and Cultural Form* (1974) that he produced or reissued during this period, lies in his extension of cultural analysis to the non-literary forms of television, advertising, and journalism, and his construction, from the expanded territory of these analyses, of a new discipline he calls "cultural materialism." This discipline arises from his growing conviction that society itself exists as "a form of communication, through which experience is described, shared, modified, and preserved," a conviction that challenges orthodox Marxism by showing "as a matter of experience, that men and societies are not confined to relationships of power, property, and production. Their relationships in describing, learning, persuading, and exchanging experiences are seen as equally fundamental."[18]

Williams dissents from the position, commonly argued by thinkers from F. R. Leavis to Theodor Adorno, that the electronic media inherently contaminate their audience. The source of that contamination, he argues, rests in minority ownership of the media, not in the technologies themselves. On the contrary, these could serve, he thinks, as a source of liberation if they could only be reallocated on a massive scale. In *Communications* and *Television*, Williams sets a "materialist" analysis exposing the unequal social arrangements that restrict ownership of the media to minority groups alongside a "cultural" program that promises to share out the instruments of communication and so achieve a richer sense of communication as means and end. As a "cultural materialist,"

Williams writes simultaneously as an observer and as a prophet, seeking both to understand existing conditions and to undermine their future force. In the end, his patient recommendations for reform, which include provision for widely diffused ownership of the means of communication and for public control of the press, owe more to the Fabian tradition of the Webbs than to either the pessimistic laments of *Scrutiny* or to the elitist cadres of European Marxism.

This unusually sympathetic attitude to postindustrial modes of communication has clearly helped to popularize Williams's approach to cultural studies. The remoteness of his theory from the more radical calls to revolutionary action makes it attractive even to liberal practitioners, while its multidisciplinary status gives it a broad appeal to institutions in which a more specialized approach would attract little support. Most important of all, the explosion of critical theory in the last decade has ensured Williams's pioneering work in "cultural materialism" a central place in any attempt to reformulate the connection between literary and social processes. In Britain, a recent collection of critical essays on Elizabethan and Jacobean dramatic literature, Jonathan Dollimore and Alan Sinfield's *Political Shakespeare* (1985), carried the subtitle *New Essays in Cultural Materialism*, as well as a subdued afterword by Williams himself. The editors have also contributed a substantial body of work in a similar vein, including Sinfield's *Literature in Protestant England 1560–1660* (1983) and *Alfred Tennyson* (1986) and Dollimore's *Radical Tragedy* (1984). Terry Eagleton's widely read *Literary Theory* (1983) and Tony Bennett's *Formalism and Marxism* (1979) both acknowledge debts to Williams's ideas. Fred Inglis's *Radical Earnestness: English Social Theory 1880–1980* (1982) emphasizes Williams's seminal importance in a tradition of cultural criticism that stretches from Ruskin to E. P. Thompson. Eugene Goodheart's *The Failure of Criticism* (1978) includes him as an exemplar of a line of twentieth-century humanist criticism alongside Trilling, Ortega y Gasset and F. R. Leavis, while Frederic Jameson's *The Political*

Unconscious (1981) places him in a radical-progressive context. Some of America's most influential cultural critics, including Alan Trachtenberg, Leo Marx, and Max Byrd, have written important review articles of his work, while his definition of the literary as a category of social production has recently gained an unexpected boost from proponents of the "new historicism."

Williams's importance as a student of popular culture and mass communications has received tribute from a variety of sources, including the British journals *Screen Education* (later *Screen*) (1958–), *Cultural Studies* (1971–1977), *Media, Culture and Society* (1979–), and the American series *Theories of Contemporary Culture* (1979–), while students of film, television, and the media, including Peter Wollen, Colin McCabe, and Terry Lovell, have all paid tribute to his work. Indeed, favorable references to his definition of literature as a category of social production abound in journals sponsored by the elite graduate schools of Berkeley, Duke, and Johns Hopkins, as well as in policy statements issued by beleaguered African institutions like the University of the Western Cape.

"Cultural Materialism" has enjoyed the succès d'estime in the 1970s and the 1980s that Williams's linkage of "culture and society" enjoyed in the late 1950s and the early 1960s. It is worth recalling, however, that his earlier work sought only to restore and to renew a tradition, while his later work aims to construct a whole intellectual field. The later Williams hopes to reform cultural theory and to update Marxism at one stroke. The same revisionist and radical impulses that he took to dramatic tradition in *Modern Tragedy* and to literary history in *The English Novel from Dickens to Lawrence* now extend to a whole politico-intellectual movement. It is no surprise, then, that as a way of reformulating cultural theory, Williams's "cultural materialism" suffers major problems. If *Marxism and Literature* and *Problems in Materialism and Culture* announced their author's new familiarity with a host of European Marxist thinkers, the books themselves manifested little protracted engagement with them. Too often, the Williams of the late 1970s and the 1980s preferred to whip his old stalking-horse, the Cambridge English faculty, whose "universalism" he attacked as if it were, indeed, the universal key to the study of all cultures its exponents pretended. Even worse, he transmitted some of his own parochialism to his British disciples. In *Radical Tragedy* and *Political Shakespeare,* Dollimore repeatedly attacks E. M. W. Tillyard's *The Elizabethan World Picture* (1943) as if it were written yesterday, while ignoring the work of European Marxists like Robert Weimann who have already covered much of his own territory. Indeed, one of Williams's more distressing legacies is this intensely provincial "universalism," the belief that the battle for cultural studies can be won on the playing fields of Cambridge.

If Williams's campaign against Cambridge English raged across many pages, he limited his battle against the new Marxist theories to a few potent asides, remaining reluctant to translate his latent misgivings into lasting analysis. Consequently, other self-professed "cultural materialists" have reduced Williams's program to little more than a slogan, harnessing it to Foucaultian or Althusserian analyses of the sort that he himself would hardly practice. Both Foucault and Althusser endorse a history without change, where "power" and an "institutional state apparatus" subdue human capacity and diversity to the fixed requirements of an authoritarian system. Williams, in contrast, reaffirmed even in his last, most pessimistic discussion of "The Uses of Cultural Theory" (*New Left Review,* 1986) that his study of culture remained stubbornly attached to the possibilities of human growth. Williams cannot, of course, be charged with the aberrations of his followers. Even so, his unwillingness to provide public grounds for his dissent from positions he nonetheless felt compelled to rebut in parentheses means that "cultural materialism" can become a label fixed to many different commodities.

Because he occupies a border country between social activism and academic caution, Williams's later reformulations of his position do not always convince. He wants literary criticism, the history of ideas, and cultural theory all to recognize their *social* quotient. This means, for instance, that he disputes the very existence of history of ideas as an independent discipline, since "it is not primarily ideas that have a history; it is societies. And then what often seem opposed ideas can in the end be seen as parts of a single social process" (*PMC*, 78). Yet although, over the years, he himself submitted many key terms of left and right to complex historical investigation, he did not extend the same suspicion to the term *social*, which he usually collapsed into *capitalist* on the one side and *common* on the other. Perhaps it was because he always remained so cautious of the word *class* that he fought shy of analyzing *social* into its component parts. Even so, it makes as little sense to say that societies have ideas as to say that ideas themselves have histories. Ideas germinate, circulate—and sometimes produce radical social conflict—among groups within societies, and these groups run across a social range from Winstanley's Diggers to the Tories of *Blackwood's Magazine* to the ever-reforming splinter groups within the British socialist left.

Because he reserves the term "class fraction" for individuals inside the Godwin circle or the Bloomsbury group whose work he personally respects, Williams tends to present such groupings as the exception rather than the norm. But it would make more sense to see the class fraction as part of the normal social process, so that an essay like his own "Ideas of Nature" (*PMC*, 1972) would become a study of a series of groups, each aiming to impress its idea on social reality. He gives notional assent to this proposal, but he never produces a detailed case study like J. G. A. Pocock's *The Machiavellian Moment* (1975) or Quentin Skinner's *The Foundations of Modern Political Thought* (1978). Williams always remained closer to Cambridge English, with its narrow range of key texts and its ideas of recurring historical crisis, than he ever liked to confess. This means that in "Ideas of Nature," for instance, he praises Basil Willey's discussion of nature, which he says "cannot

. . . be improved upon" (*PMC*, 78). Once again he stays inside Cambridge for his authority, even when Arthur Lovejoy and Joseph Warren Beach might merit at least some attention.

Finally, it is essential to remember that for Williams himself "cultural materialism" posits ends as well as means. When he first turned to Marxist cultural studies in the 1950s, he withdrew in appalled despair at the way Marxism reduced culture to an instrument for social revolution. His later work, however, reverses these priorities by calling for an end to "the old crude division between mental and manual labour" and pointing to a new social grouping that is "structurally different from the old or the new working class" (*PMC*, 271–72). Not content with withering away the classic Marxist agency of revolutionary action, he suggests that "what a society needs, before all, to produce, is as many as possible conscious individuals, capable of all necessary association" (*PMC*, 268). As Williams proceeds, "cultural materialism" comes to sound less and less like a manifesto for socialist revolution and more and more like a blueprint for educational reform. By giving a privileged place to consciousness, while suggesting that previous political and economic groupings are somehow outmoded, he inevitably redelivers himself to the reformist principles that bedeviled *Culture and Society* and *The Long Revolution*. In sum, his cultural theory repeatedly falls between two stools. As a field of study it has an altogether too problematic relationship with its inventor's socialist premises, while as a call for reform it remains too muffled by an educator's caution. Not for nothing does "The Uses of Cultural Theory" see a lost golden age for the subject in the postrevolutionary activity of the Bakhtin circle. With increasing desperation, Williams attempted to recreate in the Thatcherite Britain of the 1970s and the 1980s the fervent sense of social possibilities that marked the intellectual left in the most optimistic era of Soviet reconstruction.

V. FICTION

His cultural and political analysis of a society "Beyond Actually Existing Socialism" (*PMC*, 1980) pulls against the grain of loyalties and convictions Williams has honored throughout his career. For from the appearance of his first critical book, *Reading and Criticism* in 1950, he tried to communicate to the working class from which he himself had emerged the reading methods and cultural diagnoses pioneered by I. A. Richards and F. R. Leavis. Yet Williams's class allegiances always came across as visceral as well as cultural and political. Even when he intellectually deferred to the methods of *Scrutiny* or Richards, he always extended their point of reference outside Cambridge and the grammar schools. His best known work, the cultural trilogy consisting of *Culture and Society* (1958), *The Long Revolution* (1961), and *The Country and the City* (1973), moves from a cautious gradualism that hopes to assimilate working-class institutions into a middle-class tradition of high culture, through a bolder demand for common ownership of cultural institutions, to a militant affirmation of class identity that promises uncompromising opposition to the cultural and political status quo.

But in *Problems in Materialism and Culture* (1980) and *Culture* (1981), books written in some of the worst years for the British Parliamentary left since its formation, Williams moves in an entirely different direction, toward an endorsement of culture as the one social product capable of supporting radical change. In these books, he hopes for a cultural revolution that will capture "the real forces of production, including now especially the intellectual forces of knowledge and conscious decision" (*PMC*, 257). Unfortunately, this is a revolution in which the working classes can play only a diminished role, for their access to the means of cultural production remains drastically limited, while their structural importance in an economy increasingly organized around culture and communication dwindles almost by the day. Paradoxically, as Williams moves toward a more militant and uncompromising socialism, his cultural revolution finds less and less room for the class whose cause he originally espoused.

As a social and cultural critic, Williams has, with great reluctance, increasingly marginalized the working class. There have been exceptions—he has reminded his readers that no society can exist without the "base" provided by the producers of raw materials and agricultural products—but the later Williams looks to culture as the agency for liberation rather than to a single revolutionary group. But this is not the whole story, for the testimony of Williams the cultural critic must be placed alongside the very different testimony of Williams the novelist. As novelist, he has produced five books that compulsively return to working-class experience as elegy, critique, imaginative recreation, and eventually apotheosis. As a critic of culture, Williams banishes the working class to the margins of postindustrial production; as a novelist, he presents that class as nothing less than a guarantee of psychic health. For a critic who has repeatedly objected to the coldness of "official English culture," but who has also expressed distaste at the hardness and opportunism of organized opposition to it, the traditional life of the working class, with its settled loyalties and clearly defined obligations, offers a sharp contrast to middle-class mobility and self-estrangement. Yet Williams's working-class characters purchase this psychological tranquillity at a great price: political, and sometimes even familial, cuckolds, they are powerless to oppose the machinery of state; and what looks like solidity from one angle becomes a tomb-like immobility from another.

Nowhere does Williams's ambivalence about the historical role of the working class register more sharply than in his novels. Almost uniformly ignored by critics, *Border Country* (1960), *Second Generation* (1964), *The Volunteers* (1978), *The Fight for Manod* (1979), and *Loyalties* (1985) offer an indispensable testimony to Williams's recoil from official British culture and to his long, uneasy quest for what he calls a "settlement" with traditional working-class life. The movement back to a settled working-class community by an intellectual who has left that class recurs throughout his fiction. But where his middle-class protagonists bear the scars of alienation and self-division, his working-class communities nurture heroic figures who are nonetheless martyred by their experiences.

Such ingredients do not inspire hopes of any sudden access of impartiality in Williams's work of the kind that made Balzac so useful a commentator on nineteenth-century France, despite his overtly royalist sympathies. Even worse, they suggest that his fiction hovers on the edge of piety and sentimentalism. Not surprisingly, some critics have objected to just these qualities. Albert Hunt, for instance, describes *Loyalties* as "a socialist soap opera," while Keith Kyle has dismissed *The Volunteers* as "a religious tract."[1] Clearly, a major problem arises from the gap between Williams's intellectual recognition of the marginalization of working-class life and his almost magical faith in its restorative powers. Working-class experience is personal, collective, and productive; middle-class experience is anonymous, solitary, and manipulative. But these antitheses make for tension as well as simplification, since Williams's middle-class protagonists often see the working class as something they follow a whole social drift in leaving behind. In short, the novels become a series of increasingly anguished quests by middle-class renegades for settlement in working-class orders always on the point of supersession.

A second charge leveled against his fiction is that Williams the novelist remains a thinly disguised version of Williams the social critic. Paul Ableman, for instance, finds in *The Fight for Manod* "more rhetoric, expertise and social philosophy . . . than is compatible with artistic truth," while Stephen Wall thinks that *Second Generation* shows how "the discursive intelligence with its prophetic earnestness gets the better of the fiction."[2] Because the novels foreground employment patterns, generational conflicts, regional customs, embourgeoisement, and other typical areas of sociological interest, they have frequently been written off as the work of a sociologist manqué. But if Williams is a sociologist, he is at least an impassioned one, a C. Wright Mills rather than a Paul Lazarsfeld, one whose field is a painful self-division dramatized in terms of "the uncertainty of moving between two kinds of life" (*PL*, 273).

Williams himself always rejected any suggestion that his fiction represents an insufficiently reworked offshoot of his criticism. "The fact that I also write social criticism," he observed, "has led to a simple formula in which my novels are seen as by-products, but the two kinds of writing have always been equally important to me, and in fact the novel-writing came first and will, I think, go on longer."[3] He might have added that his fiction had already gone on longer, since his first published stories appeared in the early 1940s, several years before his first critical essay and many years before anything resembling social criticism appeared in print. The adolescent Williams wrote plays and stories, not social tracts, while the mature Williams took thirteen years and seven revisions to produce his first novel, *Border Country*. One reason for the almost glacial slowness of his fictional composition, in contrast to his fertility as a critic, is his focus on the psychological consequences of the socialist commitment. Where his criticism mainly explores the social consequences of modern alienation, his fiction focuses on personal instabilities and estrangements that are at once wider in their ramifications and more difficult to describe. His central concern as a novelist is a traditional but immensely difficult theme, the quest for a unified identity in a world that threatens and fragments the integrity of the self.

* * *

Yet Williams remains an accomplished critic of fiction as well as a novelist, and his criticism sheds useful light on his fictional concerns and techniques. Two books, *The English Novel from Dickens to Lawrence* (1970) and *Orwell* (1971), show him once again as an uncompromising adversary of "English" culture. Instead of a critical perspective that attends to individual experience, of either a sexual or an ethical nature, Williams proposes instead the problem of the "knowable community" as the main issue of British fiction. The decline of that community, and the loss of direction suffered by individuals unfortunate enough to be deprived of it, becomes the principal subject of his attention in these works, which self-consciously and even self-advertisingly declare their opposition to the metropolitan values of the academy.

The novel has always served as a vehicle for the new. But the tradition Williams erects—one that includes Dickens, Joyce, Conrad, even Wells—sets the new alongside the old in a community that moves, verbally as well as socially, between two worlds. Although he casts his net reasonably wide (his tradition remains mainly English, his internal migrants do not include Flaubert or Nabokov), Williams retains a special affection for Hardy. This is why, in *The English Novel from Dickens to Lawrence,* he defends Hardy against critics like F. R. Leavis and Lord David Cecil who present him as just another regional curiosity. Williams's Hardy, rather, occupies "that border country so many of us have been living in: between custom and education, between work and ideas, between love of place and an experience of change" (*ENDL,* 98). In Hardy's work, Williams recognized a setting he could exploit for himself, characters he could develop independently, and, most important of all, a version of his own dilemma as a writer. From his academic training he derived his ability to understand the social and historical crisis of the working class. Yet his intellectual life could neither make up for the loss of his own class roots nor provide him with a vocabulary for engaging emotionally with that loss. In the Hardy who combined "the insights of consciously learned history and of the educated understanding of nature and behaviour" with an intense attachment to "his native country, to which he is already deeply bound by memory and experience of another kind: a family and a childhood; an intense association of people and places, which has been his own history" (*ENDL*, 109), Williams glimpsed his own predicament and the possibility of shaping that predicament into fiction. Hardy provides the inspiration for some of Williams's most memorable characters and situations. The self-division of Peter Owen in *Second Generation*, the young Oxford graduate with working-class Welsh roots, has its antecedents in Hardy's Clym Yeobright; while Nesta Pritchard in *Loyalties*, the sensitive grocery store clerk and part-time painter seduced and deserted by a middle-class communist sympathizer, represents an imaginative fusion of Jude Fawley and Tess D'Urberville.

Just a year after *The English Novel from Dickens to Lawrence*, Williams turned his attention to George Orwell, the novelist who was to serve as anti-mask to his Hardy. In *Orwell* (1971), a volume in the *Modern Masters* series edited by Frank Kermode, Williams showed himself just as eager to oppose received truths as to formulate new ones. Where Hardy viewed Wessex through the eyes of a returning native, Orwell views England as an alien. In Orwell's eyes, England shrinks from a global system of class domination into an inefficient family firm. Orwell fails to confront the brutal class mechanisms that crush Jude and Tess. Instead, his proletarians become pets, by turns savage or docile. Where Hardy gives us Gabriel Oak, Orwell offers us Boxer. The only alternative he could envisage to England as an insolvent, inefficient, but lovable, Dickensian firm was the impersonal machine of Soviet totalitarianism. This was why, after an uplifting encounter with revolutionary socialism during the Spanish civil war, he returned to England to write *Animal Farm* and *1984*, books that show revolutionary governments as pathological and vengeful, and the working classes they dominate as subhuman, near animal masses.

As betrayer, Orwell stands for a whole series of ruling-class, sometime socialists who enjoy the authority extended to the ruling-class witness. This was why, after his death, he became the patron saint of neo-conservatives, repenting radicals, and the swelling ranks of those who saw in revolutionary socialism only a god that failed. Moreover, the cult of Orwell had its underside in the dehumanization of the working class. With less than absolute fairness, Williams links the later Orwell with a long line of public-school radicals—educators, labor leaders, members of parliament, media pundits, and culture heroes—who reduce the proletariat to a uniform, unthinking mass. In Orwell himself, a man whose career moved from Burmese policeman, to Spanish freedom fighter, to Hebridean exile, Williams sees a precursor for the unsettled, rootless anti-heroes of the 1950s. Orwell's shifting, perpetually mobile career convinced Williams of the value of settled, regional loyalties, so that his own fiction, with its devotion to Wales and its uncompromising socialism, becomes a tacit commentary on Orwell's achievement.

* * *

Williams's subject matter as a novelist is considerably broader than a simple list of his preoccupations might suggest. *Loyalties* alone moves from 1936 to 1984, taking in the Spanish civil war, the Normandie landings, the Suez crisis, the Grosvenor Square Vietnam demonstrations, and the 1984 miners' strike along the way. Nor does he confine himself to recording large historical crises. For all its reputed austerity, his fiction is thick with the texture of event and the clutter of social furniture, so that as a body of work it constitutes a detailed record of the changing face of British life over sixty years. In *Second Generation,* for instance, he enmeshes his characters in all the liberating machinery of the affluent 1960s, the foundation grants, the sexual politics, the mass produced motor cars, the foreign holidays, the adventure playgrounds, the coffee percolators, the "bedroom events" that anticlimactically turn into furniture sales. These are just a few, he implies, of the ways in which characters become alienated from their true potential, and in which aspirations to freedom get brutally crowded out. Our first glimpse of Matthew Price in *Border Country* establishes him as the quintessential suburbanite of the 1950s. He runs for a bus; he answers the telephone as soon as he gets through the door of his semi-detached home. Yet Williams always presses his more favored characters into an area of experience beyond "official English culture." He returns Matthew to his birthplace by having his telephone bring news of his father's stroke, which immediately transports him to a more favored source of values, his native village of Glynmawr on the Welsh border.

Williams sets working-class life at the moral center of all his fiction. Even so, the moral center cannot necessarily control everything that swarms around its rim. When *Border Country* appeared in 1960, it was immediately welcomed as an honest witness of working-class life, a reaction that overlooked some of the book's unresolved tensions. William Cooper, for instance, spoke of Williams's "evocation, passionate and inquiring," of a group of ordinary lives, while Gerda Charles in the *New Statesman* praised in particular the portrayal of Harry Price, the signalman father of Matthew Price, whose "life throughout remains undramatic, deeply independent, plain, disturbed only by the betrayals of the General Strike."[4] Certainly, *Border Country*, like all Williams's fiction, contains several such characters, figures like the platelayer Elwyn, who in carrying the young Matthew to school and the ailing Harry from his signal box attains an almost epic simplicity and grandeur. Even so, these comments push the book in the direction of a lyrical ballad rather than a novel, failing to account for its peculiar juxtaposition of past and present. Charles does not suggest how, even as Williams recreates working-class life, he shows its inevitable transformation into something estranged and anxious. When Matthew Price, the bright boy who left the valley for Cambridge, reexamines Glynmawr as an adult during a brief visit to his sick father, he notices that "the houses seemed now to stand in relation to the road, rather than to each other. It was no longer an enclosed village, but a place on the way to somewhere else, as almost everywhere in Britain was coming to be. Many of the trees under which the farms and groups of houses had sheltered were felled, and the walls seemed more open and more naked. The hedges along the road had been clipped short, and in some places replaced by stretches of wire and concrete fence."[5]

In this light, the "sense of settlement" the novel moves back into the past to retrieve becomes a settlement under stress. *Border Country* incorporates two distinct methods of narration. Its retrospective account of the Price family's original settlement in Glynmawr unfolds like a chronicle, recording distinct events in well-defined episodes. But its present-tense account of Matthew Price's fortunes as a university teacher and Welsh expatriate takes a more interior, psychological form, recreating his competing allegiances and divided loyalties with a sympathetic participation in his own scarcely veiled anxieties.

The composition of *Border Country* occupied over thirteen years of Williams's life. Arguably, no other novel he wrote came as close to his own experiences. He confessed that the two names of his hero (Matthew Price is known as "Matthew" in London and "Will" in Glynmawr) corresponded to his own double identity as "Jim" in his native village of Pandy and "Raymond" in Cambridge. Moreover, tensions and inconsistencies in the personality of his own father gave Williams the basis for the characters of Harry Price, signalman and gardener, and of his friend Morgan Rosser, entrepreneur and councillor. The description of the railway strike at Glynmawr, Williams confided, followed closely events that took place in his village of Pandy. And since Matthew Price takes Williams's route from village school to Cambridge University, the shape of the novel would seem to follow closely the shape of his own life.[6]

Yet the novel's most important feature, its steady traffic between past and present, does not rely on transcription from Williams's autobiography. Nor does the nature of that traffic remain constant throughout. At the start of the book, both past and present seem troubled, or anxious, as Matthew's tensions in an unsettling London match Harry's as a newlywed railwayman in the 1920s. Williams describes the first months of the marriage between Harry and Ellen with the same watchful unease D. H. Lawrence extends to the newly married Brangwens in *The Rainbow,* recording the same inexplicable displays of feminine tension and masculine force. As the novel continues, however, the retrospective narration serves to ease the conflict out of Glynmawr. Harry Price withdraws into unexplained self-containment, while Matthew's childhood proceeds by dramatic event—he hurls his chapel prize, a book called *The Holy Child* into the village stream; he refuses Morgan Rosser's invitation to join the management of his new factory; he trembles on the brink of a romantic entanglement with Rosser's daughter, Eira— rather than by retrospective analysis. Like her husband, Ellen Price becomes a shadowy, unfathomable figure rather than a source of marital conflict. Even Morgan Rosser, whose passage from militant to merchant Williams presents with all the patient, inward attention George Eliot extends to Silas Marner's transformation from weaver to miser, becomes in the later part of the novel a simpler creation of sudden gestures and unexplained outbursts. His ambiguous position, as socialist councillor and local entrepreneur, goes unexamined.

Instead, Williams transfers all ambiguities and uncertainties to the life of the internal migrant, the adult Matthew who fumblingly relearns how to purchase scarce goods in country districts and how to observe the proprieties of village funerals. Yet in spite of the depth of its autobiographical materials, the book lacks an important dimension, for in dividing his father's personality between two independent characters, the public servant Harry and the private capitalist Morgan, Williams takes the first step toward draining the Welsh portion of the narrative of significant conflict. Ultimately, such a split will lead to the secessionist impulses of his last novel, *Loyalties*, where he affirms the virtues of an idealized Welsh solidarity in the face of betrayals on all fronts. As it progresses, *Border Country* establishes the existence of two separate worlds, between which the troubled, uneasy Matthew Price makes his harassed migration. For the moment, however, Williams seems content to establish a radical difference between Wales and England, past and present. He has not yet sharpened this distinction into a fixed opposition.

In *Border Country*, some almost gravitational force pulls Matthew back to his Welsh roots. In the second part of Williams's Welsh trilogy, *Second Generation*, a young Welsh sociologist, Peter Owen, a city dweller of long standing, temporarily escapes to his native Wales only to be drawn back to the city by familial pressures. If the action of *Border Country* took place in a Welsh border village, the major setting for the considerably more developed conflicts of *Second Generation* is a twin industrial-academic city based on Oxford, where Williams served as a resident tutor of the university's extramural department in 1960 and 1961. His central focus rests on two very different Welsh working-class brothers who have come to work at a large car factory. One brother, Gwyn Owen, presides over a family whose contentment conceals sexual repressions and political naïveté, while just next door his brother Harold, a radical shop steward, heads a family whose political commitments rob them of personal sympathy. Harold's wife Kate works off her unfulfilled educational potential in a relationship with a bohemian don, Arthur Dean, while her son Peter gains little more than an education in disaffection from Robert Lane, his university tutor. Kate's seduction by Dean's sexual socialism parallels her son's intellectual seduction by the radical Lane. Yet despite the similarities in their situations, mother and son live like strangers in a house that serves as little more than a way station between political meetings.

In *Second Generation*, scholarships and foreign governments beckoningly entice the working-class intellectual, just as overseas holidays and consumer goods seduce his fellow workers. Indeed, none of the characters can resist the call of a "new life" that hails them from lecture hall, newspaper, and television screen. The incessant wrangling and bargaining that pervades every aspect of their present, from the marriage bed to the workplace, dissatisfies all of them. Between their hope for a new life and their disgust with the current one falls the repeated hope, voiced by almost every character, for a more "settled" existence. Yet "settled" no longer carries the same implication of stable communal living it possessed in *Border Country*. Instead, it has become a more affective matter, a projection of each character's personality and desires. For Kate Owen, settlement would mean educational and sexual fulfillment, while her son's fiancée Beth wants little more than a nuclear home and family.

In *Second Generation*, Oxford itself, unlike Glynmawr, remains a divided city. It contains motor works where the traditional industrial politics of unions versus management exhausts all concerned, and a university where socialist dons market their equally exploitative utopias. In a sense, everything seems fluid and mobile in a city where dons drop in on the houses of their students for tutorials, and where students fend off offers from American universities and third-world governments. Yet much of the novel concerns itself with hopes deferred, thwarted, and extinguished. On the shop floor, Harold Owen, perhaps the most exhausted character in the novel, must harness all his radical energies to the endless deadlock of management-labor negotiation, while the university shelters disappointed radicals like Lane, whose moralistic utopianism enervates his wife, and Dean, whose radical politics have passed into a program of sexual liberation.

Yet Williams suggests a society of almost unbearable tensions and fissures as much by omission as by inclusion. In particular, the absence of Wales as anything more than a place of retreat during a period of stress serves to lock all the characters into their intolerable working and emotional lives. In addition, *Second Generation* intensifies the atmosphere of unreasonable and overwhelming constraint by confining its action to a nine-month period and by focusing on a politicized group of characters in a society ticking on the edge of explosion into a "new life." The city that provides its setting becomes the site for a swarm of conflicting aspirations, while around its edges move the ban-the-bomb marchers whose banners suggest the explosive potential of a society that might at any time blast itself out of any settlement at all.

Second Generation repeatedly invokes a "new life" only to muffle this invocation with an equally plaintive desire for "settlement." Throughout the book, Williams plays endlessly on this, his longstanding obsession, using the word itself on not less than thirty occasions. But only in its final pages does the idea of settlement come to any point of rest, when Kate and Peter Owen, mother and son, finally confront their shrunken lives.

> "We've settled for so little, and called it normal. And then twisted body and soul to avoid seeing more. Seeing what life could really be like."
>
> "What life is like," Peter said. . . . "Because we've got this wrong, this contrast we make between potential and actual. In the end, it breaks us, because it is no way to live. If we keep reducing the present, by some idea of the future, nothing good can happen. We have to take hold where we are, and know good from bad. We've lived in this break too long. All it's taught us is breaking away. But the change will only come when we've learned to confirm."[7]

From the Owen household radiates a variety of pressures for change—sexual, political, cultural, and economic. Yet in the end the family members do little more than "confirm" an older style of life. After living in a "break," a period of personal and social upheaval, this "second generation" can think and feel nothing better than to recreate in an urban setting the more "settled" lifestyle of a generation that came before.

In *Second Generation*, Williams presents a society no

longer able to contain the aspirations of its members in the customary channels of trade unions, parliamentary socialism, and educated debate. Even so, none of the characters' radical impulses develop into anything substantial. By the end, all their impulses toward a new life have faded into air, so that the book can only close with a series of gestures. Peter Owen seems on the edge of repudiating his university career for the factory floor and a traditional family life with Beth. Kate gives up her speculations in middle-class socialism to renew working-class hearth and home with a weary Harold. In this way, the radical impulses of the characters become impoverished even before they have flared into life. For a novel written in 1964, *Second Generation* appears austerely unhopeful about the possibility of radical change. Its predominant mood is one of exhaustion, even of possible extinction, and of anger at the betrayal of working-class aspirations by middle-class speculators in socialism.

By 1979, the publication date of the third part of the trilogy, *The Fight for Manod*, the middle classes had begun to speculate in very different commodities. Williams this time elects to deal in hopes extinguished and then rekindled, a pattern that gives the book an elegiac glow. Manod, the Welsh village that provides its physical and emotional center, originally survived by subsistence farming and strategic marriages. In the late 1960s, however, government planners decided to revive it as part of a regional development program. Robert Lane, who in the late 1970s has become a senior civil servant, describes what is still merely a Whitehall project with weary cynicism as "just another new world indefinitely postponed," a hangover from a period when "there was a whole choice . . . of new worlds. On paper."[8] Lane asks Matthew Price, now a respected industrial historian, to evaluate the project, "to come to this fresh, to make it human again, to help us see it again as it is. . . . Taking with you, in yourself, the two worlds you belong in. The two Manods" (*FM*, 14).

Lane sees Manod as a corporate development in

need of Matthew's personal engagement for its survival. Yet as it unfolds, the novel discovers a multiplicity of competing Manods. For John Dance, a property speculator, "the scheme" promises just so much profitable real estate. For the young married couple, Trevor and Modlen Jenkins, it offers prospective employment and the resources of a town. For Peter Owen, released from the shop floor by a best-selling exposé of the motor industry, it provides evidence of a multinational conspiracy to exploit the area for its energy resources, while for Matthew himself it offers "a unique opportunity . . . to explore new social patterns, new actual social relations" (*FM*, 194). Manod changes shape bewilderingly, veering from "a name, a codesign, perhaps even a symbol" to "a chaos" (*FM*, 8).

Matthew alone resists these alternatives, remaining faithful to his vision of a renewal of social possibilities in a world of dwindling expectations and resources. In Manod he feels a primary bond to a place and a community, so that at the end of the book he commits himself not so much to a political process as to the essential continuity of a regional way of life. Instead of yearning for the "new life" of *Second Generation* he moves backward to the quiescence and self-containment of *Border Country*, to a settlement with nothing less than the land itself, a land that occupies

a border in the earth and in history: to north and west the great expanses of a pastoral country; to south and east, where the iron and coal had been worked, the crowded valleys, the new industries, now in their turn becoming old. There had been a contrast, once, clearly seen on this border, between an old way of life and a new, as between a father living in his old and known ways and a son living differently, in a new occupation and with a new cast of mind. But what was visible now was that both were old. The pressure for renewal, inside them, had to make its way through a land and through lives that had been deeply shaped, deeply committed, by a present that was always moving, inexorably, into the past. And those moments of the present that could connect to a future were then hard to grasp, hard to hold to, hard to bring together to a rhythm, to a movement, to the necessary shape of a quite different life. What could now be heard, momentarily, as this actual movement, had conditions of time, of growth, quite different from the conditions of any single life, or of any father and son. (*FM*, 206–7)

London may betray Wales, the Welsh may betray Wales, but only Wales can connect Matthew Price to something beyond the conflict of past and present, country and city, father and son, something almost pantheistic in its synthetic power. In a way that prefigures *The Volunteers* and *Loyalties*, Matthew makes his settlement with the land itself.

In nearly twenty years, then, Matthew Price has accomplished little more than a long march home. In the same way that *Second Generation* ended with Peter Owen returning to his father's car works, Matthew wins *The Fight for Manod* by resettling in his native region. Williams's fiction began, in *Border Country*, by dramatizing tensions, between psychology and environment, settlement and mobility, that he had also investigated more analytically in his criticism. But the trilogy itself never really adjusts to the mobility the criticism accepts as a basic premise. Williams the fiction writer always allows his characters the vacant cottage or the job opening that Williams the critic repudiated in the Victorian novelists, whose legacies and windfalls papered over insoluble conflicts in the action. It is odd that Peter Owen finds a job in the factory at a time of looming redundancy in the car industry. It is almost beyond belief that a final "radical recasting" of the Manod project should stipulate nothing more than a moderate increase in population based on a revival of agricultural wealth. One of the great virtues of realistic fiction, Williams has frequently reminded us, is its typicality. Yet his own fiction, which ignores typicality at key points in its action, often deserts realism for pastoral, for a backward movement to the simplicities of childhood and the community that is knowable only because it is so remote.

The same movement, paradoxically, informs Williams's one novel of the future, *The Volunteers* (1978). A political thriller with a psychological riddle at its heart, *The Volunteers* returns to Williams's favorite theme, the two worlds mediated by an alienated protagonist. On the one side, Britain in 1987 resembles Orwell's Oceania, with a sophisticated information technology and a well-organized ruling class concealing deep economic weaknesses. On the other side, however, lies Wales, a radically distinct region of declining heavy industry and tourist showpieces that contains, nonetheless, a mysterious saving grace. At the start of the book, Lewis Redfern, a consultant for Insatel, an international satellite news and information service, moves between these worlds with the calloused candor of Orwell's George Bowling in *Coming up for Air.* By the end, however, he has acknowledged his own roots and repudiated his cosmopolitan mores for a way of life more authentic and reserved.

The novel's central action turns on Redfern's investigation of the shooting of a coalition government minister and one-time Labour party member, Edmund Buxton. The shooting occurred during Buxton's deliberately provocative visit to a Welsh folk museum. Only four months before, he had secretly ordered troops to open fire during a strike at Pontyrhiw power station, as a result of which a young worker had died. Redfern discovers the existence of a group of activists, "the volunteers," that he links with the attack on the minister. The group's founder was Mark Evans, a Welshman who had once served alongside Buxton as a Labour junior minister, and the author of a book called *The Limits of Representative Democracy.* After Labour fell from power, Evans deserted his Welsh wife for a younger woman from London and, using his position as director of an American trust fund as a cover, formed a subversive organization designed to infiltrate and to corrode the state from within. Even so, Evans himself had no direct part in the actual attack, which had been staged by his embittered and calculating son David, a Cambridge contemporary of his second wife.

Redfern's investigation and eventual discovery of this

alienated group occupies much of *The Volunteers.* Yet the book's detective element arguably takes second place to the psychological change that overcomes Redfern as he probes deeper and deeper into Evans's mystery organization. Beyond the guerilla theater of the actual shooting—an event that, as a political consultant, he can easily accommodate to his ordinary experience—Redfern discerns something more puzzling. "The cold pleasure of the game of deception, the probably collaborative wit of the insistent false trails, had somewhere inside them an unusually hard edge: a certain settled bitterness . . . an older kind of bitterness."[9] Redfern's search for the source of this bitterness takes him a long way beyond the routine investigations he usually conducts for Insatel, forcing him to confront his own origins and their violent contradiction with what he has become. For as David Evans finds out in his own counter-investigation of the man on his father's trail, Redfern's grandparents moved to Birmingham from south Wales in their search for work, while his father died in Kenya "in one of the very worst of the last colonial wars" (*V,* 195).

In acknowledgment of these family loyalties, Redfern refuses to cooperate fully with the inquiry into the Pontyrhiw shooting. Through his connections with "the volunteers," he is able to produce the vital document in which Buxton authorized the troops to open fire. But by refusing to disclose the source of his evidence, and by deflecting his questioner from other vital points, he manages to hide the existence of Evans's "volunteers." In this way, Redfern repudiates his corporate loyalty to Insatel for a destiny obscurely linked with Wales.

Redfern makes his commitment, but the consequences of that commitment go unclarified, since he articulates them in language too numinous to translate into a social program.

> To be there and to be telling it was a local moment, a significant moment, but the immense process continued and there was no available identity outside it: only the process itself, which could never be properly told in any single dimension or

any single place. There was only, now, the deep need to connect and the practical impossibility, for unregrettable reasons,
of making the connections, even the known connections. Yet
then, all the time, within this impossibility, were the inevitable commitments, the necessary commitments, the choosing
of sides. (*V*, 207)

His reflections are almost as vague as Wordsworth's
"sense sublime / Of something far more deeply inter-
fused." In fact, when a Welsh protester, the brother-in-law
of the miner who was shot, stands up in court to denounce
the minister, Redfern feels a "sense of strangeness, of
some other kind of being. It was a voice from beyond the
existing formal relations" (*V*, 203). Because he describes
the whole event in terms of an almost spiritual election, a
grace unprecedentedly extended to a cosmopolitan sin-
ner, he invests the processes of protest and oppression
with transcendent significance, transporting both his
own actions and the book's central conflict entirely outside the political realm.

Redfern's testament completes the picture Williams's
novels have built up since *Border Country.* In many ways,
Williams is a disturbingly simple writer, always distribut-
ing moral worth in inverse proportion to social and regional status. Although Redfern's final goal remains obscure, Williams's own picture is strikingly clear. His Wales
has seceded morally and socially from an England that
betrays it on all fronts. His Wales does not harbor any violence: the book's only two acts of violence originate in an
impersonal, hard London. (Exiles from the working-class
community and middle-class renegades, not native
Welshmen, shoot the class enemy Buxton in *The Volunteers.*) All hope of purity and personal integration, he
implies, depends on the relinquishment of metropolitan
identity. Williams does not present the volunteers as a
commendable group of characters, yet his eagerness to
divide the state into two separate economic and ethical
realms seems as uncompromisingly radical in its implications as anything they themselves could conjure up.

The Wales of Williams's later fiction becomes not so

much exemplary as autonomous. In *The Fight for Manod* and *The Volunteers*, Wales does not, as in *Border Country*, embody social relationships that other groups could imitate. The Pontyrhiw of *The Volunteers* does not stand for a "knowable community" so much as a way of life to which an individual must be born. It is as if, from the ruins of an Orwellian dystopia, Williams tried to create his own version of a Welsh pastoral. In *Loyalties*, however, he attempts the even more ambitious task of updating Disraeli's two nations. On one front, he describes a Wales repeatedly driven back on its own moral resources. On the other, he describes a metropolis that for nearly fifty years has spun ever more elaborate webs of surveillance and subterfuge. At the start of the book, a private coal industry has assigned spies to keep an eye on potential protesters. By its end a Conservative government has knighted the civil servant who helped them to win their class war while passing their secrets to the Russians.

Once again, Williams weaves together a seam of interlocking stories that combine elements of espionage and mystery with working-class chronicle. At the start of the book in 1936, Nesta Pritchard, a Welsh working-class girl with artistic abilities, meets Norman Braose, an upper middle-class Cambridge graduate with communist sympathies, at a political rally. A seduction inevitably occurs, after which they both withdraw behind their respective class lines: Nesta to part-time painting and marriage to Bert Lewis, a wounded communist miner and union organizer; Norman to espionage, computer research, and marriage to a vacuous but refined hostess. However, the product of their union, Gwyn, cannot withdraw quite so easily. He is sent, with the help of Norman's communist sister Emma, to Cambridge and then to employment in a government research institute. At first Gwyn's future seems reasonably settled, but when his application for promotion triggers some unwelcome political questions and the attentions of office spies, he begins to question his loyalty to a state that so casually infringes the civil liberties of its subjects in the interests of national security.

In fact, Gwyn's divided identity represents something Wales alone can heal. Returning to his mother during the miners' strike of 1984, he acknowledges the regional loyalties they share:

> "Dic's got his duty, you understand that?"
> "Of course."
> "Down here we stand by each other."
> "I know, Mam. You don't have to tell me."[10]

Against Nesta's complex web of regional commitments, Williams places the image of Norman Braose, now knighted, a retired civil servant withdrawn into a country-house world of nature conservation. "In that wood," he tells his son, "I learn more in an hour than in all the labelled, alienated arguments of the world. And I put myself in relation to it, understanding reason and civilisation in quite new ways" (L, 363). For Norman, nature alone contains the possibilities of reciprocity Nesta finds in community life. The juxtaposition ensures that Williams's own convictions scarcely need voicing. The gap between her commitment to a shared human present and his lofty legacy to a faceless future decisively registers the distinction between working- and middle-class radicalism. In Loyalties, the working classes seem ethically superior to the systems they oppose, while the middle classes appear at best ethically indifferent or undeveloped.

But Loyalties moves beyond Gwyn's quest for identity and Norman's betrayal of his militant youth to a larger historical and social canvas. The story starts on the eve of the Spanish civil war and ends in 1984 as the miners face defeat. In Spain, Bert Lewis accepts a pair of binoculars from Paul Howe, a Cambridge graduate who has joined the loyalist forces. Paul later dies in battle, while Bert himself is seriously wounded in Normandie. Throughout the novel, Williams implies that survival on anything other than working-class terms inevitably taints and compromises. His repudiation of anything other than grass-roots socialism and his myth of a homogeneous working class betrayed by metropolitan sophistication now become complete. In a book supplied with all the machinery of a historical novel—the important dates and incidents, the authentic detail, the appropriate factions—what remains most surprising is Williams's lack of historical imagination. His own mythical pattern of working-class suffering and middle-class scheming bears more resemblance to the Soviet realism of Maxim Gorki's *Mother* than to the novels of Dickens, Hardy, and George Eliot his own criticism so imaginatively dissects.

Williams attacked Orwell for the myth of family unity he fabricated to conceal the fact of class division in Britain. Yet his own later fiction simplified historical reality in equally damaging ways. Only a rousing chorus of civic virtue and self-help rings out from the mining communities described in *Loyalties*. All that keeps these communities together are the primary virtues apparent in Williams's title, a common but declining way of earning a living, and a fierce antagonism toward "the enemy" that miraculously never spills out into class hatred. Williams even presents the 1984 miners' strike—one of the most violent clashes in recent British history—as an exercise in working-class solidarity. Similarly, in Grosvenor Square, during the anti-Vietnam demonstrations of 1968, a nasty policeman stands on a female protestor's foot. The chivalrous Dic Lewis, Gwyn's half-brother, rises to her defense and gets jailed for his trouble. One sometimes longs for a really loathsome working-class character to appear in Williams's novels.

But of course more serious objections remain. What, for instance, is the psychological price of the social uniformity the residents of Wales need to prosecute their fight against government pit closures? How representative of other working-class groups are the Welsh communities that Williams sets at the center of his fictions? These are questions that he seems more willing to confront as a social critic than as a novelist. Perhaps one should see the later novels, with their strident oversimplifications, as the festive comedies of an exhausted—or of a completely despairing—social critic.

The extent of Williams's alienation from metropolitan and intellectual culture can be measured by the long march of his fiction from the anguished realism of *Second Generation*, where no single character escaped alienation, to the militant pastoral of *The Volunteers*, where psychological alienation contained the seeds of social renewal, to *Loyalties*, where for the virtuously defeated proletariat alienation has disappeared alongside victory. Williams's later novels compensate for a cultural analysis that withers away the working class by a narrative that apotheosizes it. The "knowable community," the small-scale society threatened by change, that provides the moral center of his criticism becomes the hero of a fiction in which social change and moral corruption work hand in hand. Williams's novels serve ends more sectarian than his cultural criticism. As a novelist, he has always relied on the small audience that is prepared to trade complex interconnections for a high level of class militancy.

VI. CONCLUSION

WILLIAMS'S later work suffers from the occupational hazard of the alienated mind, an increasing marginalization. His last two novels betray this potentially self-defeating hostility to metropolitan intellectuals (his most likely audience, after all) and a loyalty to a working class that he sets in almost the same kind of "enamelled world" he deplored in Renaissance pastoral poetry. In his ambitious body of fiction, one senses some measure of estrangement not imaginatively worked through. In the 1980s, too, he compulsively returned to old critical material, so that his seemingly endless rehearsals of the fortunes of Cambridge English and the reputation of F. R. Leavis display some of the later Leavis's own withdrawal into intransigent private obsessions.

Even so, the Williams of the 1980s remained a far from spent force. Two late works, *Towards 2000* (1983) and "The Uses of Cultural Theory" (1986), interweave his strengths and limitations in a way that invites a more general assessment of his stature and achievement. Indeed, the publication history of both works points to his undiminished status in postwar British intellectual life. *Towards 2000*, which combines material that first appeared in *New Left Review* and *London Review of Books*, displays his willingness to recruit from the broadest cultural base. Some of his more occult statements of Marxist theory have made it easy to overlook this aspect of his work, which has led him to explore every avenue for his message from the BBC to the socialist *Tribune*, the communist *Daily Worker*, the liberal *Guardian*, and the bipartisan *Listener* and *Times Higher Education Supplement*. The second work, "The Uses of Cultural History," delivered as a lecture to "Oxford University Limited," an alliance of students and faculty formed in the early 1980s to press for syllabus reform, once again proves his remarkable versatility. For Williams not only maintained his status as a charismatic hero for the intellectual left some forty years after his first appearance, but also functioned as a tireless reformer, the veteran of endless academic and cultural committees. Far from excluding himself from the life of his times, he helped to formulate reports on everything from public broadcasting to authors' lending rights, as well as serving on a host of Cambridge college and departmental committees.

But Williams's stature in British intellectual life rested on his arguments as well as on his reputation. Among his later works, *Towards 2000* suggests most clearly how formidable a figure he became in his later years. In its range and conviction, this, the last in a line of imaginatively organized cultural diagnoses, points to his status as critic, radical socialist, and passionate utopian. Written in a more popular idiom than his other late theoretical collections (perhaps Cobbett, to whom he devoted a *Past Masters* monograph in the same year, may bear some of the credit for this), *Towards 2000* branches from Williams's personal past to some possible futures for the society of the millennium. He begins his book with a defense of utopian thinking and moves back to his own predictions for Britain in the 1960s (reprinted verbatim from *The Long Revolution*) before analyzing the social structures and foreign policies of representative western democracies. His final chapter, "Resources for a Journey of Hope," outlines two alternative attitudes toward the future: one that exploits available material and human resources in order to preserve its own power; and one that conserves present resources with the needs of an egalitarian future explicitly in mind.

One of the chief strengths of *Towards 2000* lies in its willingness to confront the future head on. At a time when socialists from Louis Althusser to C. Wright Mills favor the backward glance, when even Alasdair MacIntyre betrays some nostalgia for the age of Jane Austen, Williams's bearings seem decisively set for the future. He looks at the future with a rational eye, seeing in postin-

117

dustrial society neither Messianic possibilities nor a barren track into a microchip dystopia. Instead, he thinks that new developments in media technology and information retrieval, if accompanied by the necessary changes in ownership and distribution, could offer indispensable assistance to the growth of a participatory democracy. To replace what he calls "the socialist command economy," he urges the revival of "a sharing society" (*TT*, 101), where "the one great area of work that will never be made redundant, though it may continue to gain useful technical supports, is in the nurture and lifelong care of people" (*TT*, 91). In other words, Williams does not restrict his definition of productive work to the production of commodities or even of ideas. Radical thinking has too often wrapped itself in the iron laws of capital to extend too much charity to its victims, which means that one of Williams's most significant contributions to the socialist tradition in *Towards 2000* lies in his unusual combination of progressive analysis and sympathetic human understanding. The work impressively combines a sustained opposition to existing society with some imaginative sketches of a more compassionate alternative. Williams matches the indignation of Alasdair MacIntyre's *After Virtue* to the compassion of Richard Titmuss's *The Gift Relationship*.

The book's second strength comes from Williams's ability to compile and to annihilate an ensemble of current clichés about Britain in the 1980s. This leads him to ask what lies behind statements such as "the present is an era of limits" and "a mixed economy provides the only basis for a democracy." This leads him to question the belief that "parliamentary democracy, as we know it" stands at the outermost limit of national aspiration. Williams accepts none of these formulations. If the present marks an era of limits, he argues, then the limits must refer to capitalist greed, not to the expectations of the underprivileged. A social policy rather than an economic model, however accommodating, must form the basis of any party with aspirations to social justice. And faith in

118

"parliamentary democracy, as we know it" ignores a network of expedients, from ministerial patronage to organized lobbying, that have little to do with either parliament or democracy. In other words, the Williams who recoiled in disgust from the machinery of government in "A Letter from the Country" and "Public Inquiry" returns in *Towards 2000* to confront its slogans with sociological and polemical skill. The cultural lexicon assembled in *Keywords* proves remarkably useful in destroying the platitudes of a marketing democracy sponsored by Saatchi & Saatchi.

When Williams moves in his last chapter to the prospects for a radical socialist future, his critical powers do not desert him. He channels the moral disgust that has, since the time of R. H. Tawney and Christopher Caudwell, become almost traditional in British radical thought into a sustained analysis of the psychological and political forces that are destroying Britain's collective future, and, alternatively, the educational and social institutions that represent "the real bases from which cooperative relationships can grow" (*TT*, 267). He identifies as his enemy a congeries of destructive forces he labels as "Plan X," a potpourri of social Darwinism, laissez-faire capitalism, and postcolonial imperialism that barters the future in the greed of the moment. Beginning with the addictive dependencies and other forms of self-abuse that destroy so many contemporary personal and social relationships, he moves progressively outward, showing the same destructive forces at work in the marketplace, in the environment, and in politics as a whole. What he proposes instead is a "shift from 'production' to 'livelihood': from an alienated generality to direct and practical ways of life" (*TT*, 267). To achieve this crucial shift in consciousness we need to develop a view of the future—and of human nature—focused on "a fundamental sense of the necessary connections with nature and of these connections as interactive and dynamic" (*TT*, 263). Like John Berger, another committed yet strangely meditative radical thinker, Williams sees human beings as agencies of growth rather than as units of consumption. Like Berger, too, he indicates the importance of earnestness for the British cultural critic, an earnestness that displaces the exegetical ingenuity of a Frederic Jameson or a Roland Barthes. Even critics who reject Williams's findings still prize the seriousness of his inquiries, as the very different testimonies of Richard Wollheim and E. P. Thompson make clear.[1]

Indeed, Williams suffered from no shortage of any kind of tribute. Anthony Giddens spoke of his "sustained commitment to the long revolution towards a participatory socialism" as "a source of inspiration to everyone interested in radical social change." Anthony Barnett suggested that "Raymond Williams stands for a kind of *truthfulness*," an assessment echoed by Fred Inglis, who described his work as standing "in lonely monumentality, profoundly serious, scathing, patriotic and, most unusual of all, adequate both to the times and to the enemy." As Blake Morrison remarked, Williams took over from F. R. Leavis for a whole generation of British writers.[2] For the left he provided an inspirational example. For anyone writing on modern British culture he became an almost mandatory citation.

Yet however secure his exemplary status, surprisingly little extended analysis has appeared of Williams's character and work. Once again *Towards 2000* may help to suggest why. On occasions, his seriousness degenerated into ponderousness, into the uniform solemnity of a prose that seems to raise agents, relationships, and events to its own imperious level of abstraction.

> The necessary new position is that this orientation to the world as raw material necessarily includes an attitude to people as raw material. It is this use and direction of actual majorities of other people as a generalised imput of "labour" which alone makes possible the processes of generalised capital and technology. Thus the drive to use the earth as raw material has involved, from the beginning, the practical subordination of such majorities by a variety of means. . . . The system of capitalist property and wage relations is only one such form. . . .

What is most at issue is the basic orientation itself, in which relations to other people and to the physical world have changed and developed in a connected process, within which the variations are important but neither absolute nor, in our present situation, decisive. (*TT*, 261)

Some of Williams's fellow writers on the left, such as E. P. Thompson and Jean-Paul Sartre, resorted to the tactics of the pillory, vilifying their opponents at length and in specific detail. Williams never pilloried, but he could sometimes confuse. He would, in fact, go to almost any lengths not to identify his targets. The "orientation to the world as raw material," he notes, originates among "military, political, economic, ideological" groups (*TT*, 261), a classification that manages to cover all its bases without actually identifying any of them.

Similarly, his oblique reference to a "connected process" invests capitalism with almost totemic force, making it a system too awesome to address directly. By equating our basic "orientation to the world as raw material" with "a drive" or "a more fundamental level of decision" (*TT*, 261), he inevitably presents capitalism in volitional rather than political terms, so that it seems to disappear even as he describes it. Of course, his lack of specificity did serve its own polemical purposes. By refusing to identify his opposition and by streamlining his argument to a few self-supplied abstractions he rarely expanded by quotations, he avoided the turmoil of public debate. In its unwillingness to pinpoint its targets or even to allow them the benefit of quotation, his style carries off the unlikely coup of making the apocalyptic sound soothing.

It seems unlikely, however, that Williams's work will stand or fall by its stylistic or rhetorical resources. He must be understood finally, as R. P. Bilan has pointed out, as the author of "the first important body of socialist literary-cultural criticism to come out of England."[3] Except for the early dramatic work, which followed the methods of Leavis, Knights, and *Scrutiny*, Williams's literary criticism served the cause of his socialism. He expanded the 270 page *Drama from Ibsen to Eliot* into the 400 page *Drama from Ibsen to Brecht* by intensifying his political commitments as much as by expanding his range of plays. A deeply felt conviction of the forces that imprison the individual in society provides the governing principle behind the second work, whereas the first simply extends Eliot's prejudices about the drama to the European naturalist tradition.

Of course, Williams's social vision sometimes distorted his literary criticism. The determination to read the Brontës as social novelists proves as unprofitable in *The English Novel from Dickens to Lawrence* as it does in Arnold Kettle's *An Introduction to the English Novel* (1951). In *The Country and the City* (1973), a work that combines social history with literary criticism in unpredictable ways, Williams's testy asides on Robert Herrick and Ben Jonson provide the sort of provocative misreading that only a major critic can afford to make. Where he failed to make contact with a particular "structure of feeling"—a rhythm of personal obsessions in his subject that corresponds to some larger social crisis or ideological fissure—his criticism lacks all conviction. But when he could match an author's obsessions to his own—Ibsen's concern with inherited debt, Hardy's compulsive return to the tensions of the internal migrant, alienated but indebted to the culture that reared him—Williams's criticism becomes moving and powerful.

As a cultural critic, his achievement would seem difficult to surpass. Along with Richard Hoggart, Williams was one of the first writers to suggest that cultural criticism could be written from a working-class perspective. Like Hoggart, he showed that working-class life provided its own "settlements," its own unions, clubs, and recreational forms, its own distinctive assumptions and aspirations. As a champion of working-class culture, Williams will probably always appeal most strongly to British audiences. Even so, his socialism recognizes the existence of a variety of cultural forms with a varying relationship to middle-class institutions. Unlike Hoggart, he came to grips with the fact that a modern society characterized by extreme social mobility will necessarily experience a variety of cultures, some of which will reinforce middle-class norms, some of which will bitterly contest them, and some of which will bypass them entirely. This is why he insisted on understanding culture in something more than class terms, as a form of communication, a web of intersecting patterns of social behaviour and valuation that governs everything from Sophocles's *Oedipus Rex* to BBC Television's *Softly Softly*.

This means, in turn, that it has become more common since Williams's own studies to view culture in institutional as well as in literary terms, so that its organization, membership, recruitment, and transmission become social facts susceptible to sociological methods of inquiry. And because Williams's equation between culture and communication derives from research that he conducted in the United States and in Europe, it appeals to critics in other countries and disciplines. Without the innovations that Williams offered in *The Long Revolution* (1961) and *Marxism and Literature* (1977), studies like Jerome McGann's *The Romantic Ideology* (1983) and *The Beauty of Inflections* (1985) and Gerald Graff's *Professing Literature* (1987) might not have appeared, or might have taken the severely doctrinal form of Louis Althusser's "Ideology and Ideological State Apparatuses" (1969), in which every aspect of cultural life becomes subservient to ruling-class power and ideology. Williams rarely allowed his socialist commitments to crowd out empirical investigation, and because he saw culture as a more diverse and liberating experience than Althusser or Marx himself, his work appeals to critics of various ideological hues.

The last point to consider is Williams's status as a revolutionary socialist. In *Politics and Letters*, he reinterpreted his whole career from such a perspective, while in *Problems in Materialism and Culture, Marxism and Literature,* and *Towards 2000*, he showed a sophisticated awareness of the state as an institution of dominance and control in the interests of the market. On the surface, his credentials as a revolutionary, a British Sartre, would appear impeccable. Yet such an impression would radically mislead, for Williams's tense, brooding ruminations on key words like *culture* and *communication* lack the sharp interplay of opposing terms that the dialectic as employed by Lukács or Sartre makes immediately available to the Marxist critic. In Williams's work, words accrete meaning across history; in Marxist criticism, meanings polarize and unite according to a preexisting intellectual scheme. Nor does Williams share Marx's or Lukács's idea of proletarian life as a condition of absolute poverty. On the contrary, an idealized working-class experience dominates Williams's criticism, fiction, and drama. As a result, he shows a marked reluctance to confront the means by which an industrial society channels power, authority, and knowledge to a few. For Williams, the arrival of a postindustrial society must have proved a gift from God, for throughout his career he criticized industrial society from the perspective of the dispossessed and the estranged. He never, in other words, analyzed that society from the perspective of its controllers. At best, this absence meant that he could register a principled disengagement from the industrial order. At his worst, it meant that he offered a long revolution that became a bloodless version of Marx's impassioned utopianism.

Towards 2000, where he sketches the substance of an alternative social order, illustrates his virtues and limitations as a social thinker. For, as Williams presents it, the ideal society would rest on "bonding," the kind of affective and kinship ties between individuals and groups that he remembered from his own Welsh past. "Bonding" becomes so important a concept for Williams that he can reduce the United States to the formulaic statement that it is a society "with unique problems of bonding" (*TT,* 170). In the bonds of region, family, and environment, he finds "the sources of a different ethos . . . those ultimately deeper attachments and purposes, which capitalism tries to push into a lower importance, or where necessary to cancel" (*TT,* 171).

Once again he voices his convictions in a language

nearer to Wordsworth than to Marx. On the one side the heart's "deeper attachments and purposes"; on the other side the repressive machinery of state capitalism: it seems no accident that Williams distinguishes these spheres so sharply, since he never really conquered his unacknowledged inheritance from *Scrutiny,* an intellectual's alienation from the marketplace, a realm he mainly presented as a Manichaean diversion from "our deeper attachments and purposes."

The source of Williams's radicalism lies here, in his deep-felt belief that primary bonds and regional roots offer a seedbed for social justice. Although his distinguished career took him far from Wales, he invested more and more commitment in an outsider's socialism. In other words, his Welsh experience determined the course of his later alliances with "people to the left . . . of the French and Italian communist parties, the German and Scandinavian comrades, the communist dissidents from the East" (*PL,* 296). Williams always offered his public a dissident's socialism, a socialism stubbornly opposed to the seductions of the marketplace or the power of the organized party. Following his death early in 1988, his work must meet its greatest test. As memories fade of the man himself, will his testimony continue to make its impact on an intellectual community that quickly forgets its last adversarial challenge? Those who share Williams's misgivings about a global political and economic system regulated mainly by greed and power, those who look with the same misgivings at a socialism unacquainted with the working classes it originally took to liberate, will hope that his long career in opposition sustains many similar "journeys of hope."

NOTES

Notes to Chapter I: Introduction

1. *My Cambridge* (London: Robson, 1984), 55.

2. *The English Novel from Dickens to Lawrence* (London: The Hogarth Press, 1984), 191. Cited hereafter as *ENDL* in text.

3. *Marxism and Literature* (Oxford: Oxford University Press, 1977), 4–5. Cited hereafter as *ML* in text.

4. *Modern Tragedy* (London: Verso Editions, 1979), 209–10. Cited hereafter as *MT* in text.

5. *Politics and Letters* (London: New Left Books and Verso Editions, 1979), 66. Cited hereafter as *PL* in text.

6. *Writing in Society* (London: Verso Editions, 1983), 22. Cited hereafter as *WS* in text.

7. *The Long Revolution* (Harmondsworth: Penguin Books, 1965), 375. Cited hereafter as *LR* in text.

8. *Towards 2000* (Harmondsworth: Penguin Books, 1985), 239. Cited hereafter as *TT* in text.

9. *The Country and the City* (London: The Hogarth Press, 1985), 84. Cited hereafter as *CC* in text.

10. *Keywords* (London: Fontana Paperbacks, 1983), 33, 36.

11. "A Dialogue on Actors," *The Critic* 1, 1 (1947): 17–24 (22).

12. *Orwell* (London: Fontana/Collins, 1971), 53. Cited hereafter as *O* in text.

Notes to Chapter II: Drama

1. Terry Eagleton, "Criticism and Politics: The Work of Raymond Williams," *New Left Review* 95 (1976): 3–23 (19–20); J. P. Ward, *Raymond Williams* (Cardiff: University of Wales Press, 1981), 28; Stuart Hampshire, "Unhappy Families," *New Statesman,* 29 July 1966, 169–70; Frank Kermode, "Tragedy & Revolution," *Encounter,* August 1966, 83–85 (84).

2. "A Dialogue on Actors," *The Critic* 1, 1 (1947): 17–24 (22).

3. *Drama from Ibsen to Eliot* (London: Chatto and Windus, 1954), 12. Cited hereafter as *DIE* in text.

4. L. C. Knights, "How Many Children Had Lady Macbeth?" in *Explorations* (London: Chatto and Windus, 1946), 1–39 (18).

5. "Four Elizabethan Dramatists: A Preface to an Unwritten Book," in *Selected Essays,* 2d ed. (London: Faber and Faber, 1934), 109–17 (111).

6. "A Dialogue on Dramatic Poetry," in *Selected Essays,* 43–58 (46); "Four Elizabethan Dramatists," 110.

7. "A Dialogue on Actors," 22.

8. *Drama from Ibsen to Brecht* (Harmondsworth: Penguin Books, 1973), 118–19. Cited hereafter as *DIB* in text.

9. *Modern Tragedy* (London: Chatto and Windus, 1966), 259.

10. Ibid., 250.

11. "A Letter from the Country," *Stand* 12, 2 (1970–1971): 17–34 (27).

12. Ibid., 18, 31, 33.

13. Ibid., 25, 34.

14. "Public Inquiry," *Stand* 9, 2 (1967): 15–53 (31).

15. Ibid., 17.

16. Ibid., 50.

17. Ibid., 50.

Notes to Chapter III: Culture

1. Frank Kermode, "Burke to Orwell," *Encounter,* January 1959, 86–88 (86).

2. Maurice Cranston, review of *Culture and Society, London Magazine,* May 1959, 60–62 (62); E. P. Thompson, "The Long Revolution," *New Left Review* 9 (1961): 24–33 (24); Asa Briggs, "Creative Definitions," *New Statesman,* 10 March 1961, 386 and 390 (386).

3. Anonymous, "Notes Towards the Definition of What?" *Times Literary Supplement,* 10 March 1961, 147; Richard Hoggart, "An Important Book," *Essays in Criticism* 9 (1959): 171–79 (175); Dwight Macdonald, "Looking Backward," *Encounter,* June 1961, 79–84 (80).

4. *Culture and Society 1780–1950* (New York: Harper & Row, 1966), 337. Cited hereafter as *CS* in text.

5. "For Continuity in Change," *Politics and Letters* 1, 1 (Summer 1947): 3–5 (3).

6. "Sociology and Literature," *Scrutiny* 13 (1945): 74–81 (80).

7. "Culture and Crisis," *Politics and Letters* 1, nos. 2 and 3 (Winter-Spring 1947–1948): 5–8 (7).

8. "Dali, Corruption and His Critics," *Politics and Letters* 1, nos. 2 and 3 (Winter-Spring 1947–1948): 112–13 (113).

9. "The Function of Criticism at the Present Time," *Essays in Criticism* 3 (1953): 1–27 (13, 19).

10. "The Idea of Culture," *Essays in Criticism* 3 (1953): 239–66 (239, 241).

11. See "Figures and Shadows," *Highway,* February 1954, 169–72 (170); "Standards," *Highway,* December 1954, 43–46; "Class and Classes," *Highway,* January 1956, 84–86; "A Kind of Gresham's Law," *Highway,* February 1958, 107–110.

12. *Lawrence* (London: Fontana/Collins, 1973), 100–101.

Notes to Chapter IV: Socialism

1. Max Byrd, "City Lights," *Partisan Review* 41 (1974): 132–37 (132).

2. "The Accents of Raymond Williams," *Critical Quarterly* 26 (1984): 47–57.

3. *The Function of Criticism: From the Spectator to Post-Structuralism* (London: Verso Editions, 1984), 109.

4. *Problems in Materialism and Culture* (London: Verso Editions, 1980), 20. Cited hereafter as *PMC* in text.

5. "Ideology and Ideological State Apparatuses," in *Lenin and Philosophy and Other Essays* (London: New Left Books, 1971), 129.

6. *The Order of Things: An Archaeology of the Human Sciences* (New York: Vintage Books, 1973), 387.

7. *The Meaning of Contemporary Realism* (London: Merlin Press, 1963), 32, 75, 20.

8. "A Letter on Art," in *Lenin and Philosophy and Other Essays*, 204.

9. "The Work of Art in the Age of Mechanical Reproduction," in *Illuminations,* edited by Hannah Arendt (New York: Schocken Books, 1969), 221, 231.

10. *Considerations on Western Marxism* (London: New Left Books, 1976), 54.

11. *Cultural Creation in Modern Society* (Saint Louis: Telos Press, 1976), 50, 32, 49.

12. *Problems of Dostoevsky's Poetics,* edited by Caryl Emerson, introduced by Wayne C. Booth (Theory and History of Literature, Volume 8) (Minneapolis: University of Minnesota Press, 1984), 32.

13. "Culture is Ordinary," in *Conviction,* edited by Norman Mackenzie (London: MacGibbon and Kee, 1958), 74–92.

14. *Culture* (London: Fontana Paperbacks, 1981), 74. Cited hereafter as *C* in text.

15. *Criticism and Ideology: A Study in Marxist Literary Theory* (London: Verso Editions, 1978), 125–26.

16. Introduction to *Hard Times* (Harmondsworth: Penguin Books, 1969), 25. Reprinted in *The Real Foundations: Literature and Social Change* (London: Chatto and Windus, 1973), 109–31.

17. "Problematical," *New Statesman,* 19 August 1977, 248–49 (248).

18. *Communications,* 3d edition (Harmondsworth: Penguin Books, 1976), 10.

Notes to Chapter V: Fiction

1. Albert Hunt, "Socialist Soap," *New Society,* 27 September 1985, 460; Keith Kyle, "Insatel Man," *Listener,* 31 August 1978, 286–87 (286).

2. Paul Ableman, "Sociofiction," *Spectator,* 27 January 1979, 23; Stephen Wall, "With Whip and Junk," *Listener,* 3 December 1964, 913.

3. Quoted in James Vinson, ed., *Contemporary Novelists* (London: Macmillan, 1982), 696–97.

4. William Cooper, "New Novels," *Listener,* 1 December 1960, 1017; Gerda Charles, "New Novels," *New Statesman,* 19 November 1960, 800–801 (800).

5. *Border Country* (Harmondsworth: Penguin Books, 1964), 292–93.

6. See the chapter entitled "The Welsh Trilogy; *The Volunteers,*" in *Politics and Letters,* 271–302.

7. *Second Generation* (London: Chatto and Windus, 1964), 338–39.

8. *The Fight for Manod* (London: Chatto and Windus, 1979), 9, 8. Cited hereafter as *FM* in text.

9. *The Volunteers* (London: The Hogarth Press, 1985), 64. Cited hereafter as *V* in text.

10. *Loyalties* (London: Chatto and Windus, 1985), 349. Cited hereafter as *L* in text.

Notes to Chapter VI: Conclusion

1. Richard Wollheim, "The English Dream," *Spectator,* 10 March 1961, 334–35; E. P. Thompson, "The Long Revolution," *New Left Review* 9 (1961): 24–33; "The Long Revolution—II," *New Left Review* 10 (1961): 34–39.

2. Anthony Giddens, "Raymond Williams' Long Revolution," *Times Higher Education Supplement,* 14 December 1979, 11–12 (12); Anthony Barnett, "Raymond Williams and Marxism: A Rejoinder to Terry Eagleton," *New Left Review* 99 (1976): 47–64 (55); Fred Inglis, "Innocent at Home," *New Society,* 27 October 1983, 158–60 (159); Blake Morrison, "The Wise Womb," *New Statesman,* 19 January 1979, 88.

3. R. P. Bilan, "Raymond Williams: From Leavis to Marx," *Queen's Quarterly* 87 (1980): 211–23 (211).

WORKS BY RAYMOND WILLIAMS

Novels

Border Country. London: Chatto and Windus, 1960; New York: Horizon Press, 1962.

Second Generation. London: Chatto and Windus, 1964; New York: Horizon Press, 1965.

The Volunteers. London: Eyre Methuen, 1978; Topsfield, Mass.: Salem House Publishers, 1986.

The Fight for Manod. London: Chatto and Windus, 1979.

Loyalties. London: Chatto and Windus, 1985; Topsfield, Mass.: Salem House Publishers, 1987.

Plays

"Koba," in *Modern Tragedy* (first edition only). London: Chatto and Windus, 1966.

"A Letter from the Country" (televised April 1966). Revised version published in *Stand* 12, 2 (1970–1971): 17–34.

"Public Inquiry" (televised March 1967). Published in *Stand* 9, 1 (1967): 15–53.

Criticism

Reading and Criticism. London: Frederick Muller, 1950.

Drama from Ibsen to Eliot. London: Chatto and Windus, 1952; New York: Oxford University Press, 1953. Revised edition, Harmondsworth: Penguin, 1964. Revised as *Drama from Ibsen to Brecht.* London: Chatto and Windus, 1968; New York: Oxford University Press, 1969.

Drama in Performance. London: Frederick Muller, 1954. Chester Springs, Penn.: Defour Editions, 1961. Revised edition, London: C. A. Watts, 1968. New York: Basic, 1969.

Preface to Film, with Michael Orrom. London: Film Drama, 1954.

Culture and Society 1780–1950. London: Chatto and Windus and New York: Columbia University Press, 1958. Reprinted, with postscript, Harmondsworth: Penguin, 1963.

The Long Revolution. London: Chatto and Windus and New York: Columbia University Press, 1961.

Communications. Harmondsworth and Baltimore: Penguin Books, 1962. First revised edition, London: Chatto and Windus, 1966; New York: Barnes and Noble, 1967. Second revised edition, Harmondsworth: Penguin, 1976.

The Existing Alternatives to Communication. London: Fabian Society, 1962.

Modern Tragedy. London: Chatto and Windus and Stanford: Stanford University Press, 1966. Revised edition, London: Verso Editions, 1979.

The English Novel from Dickens to Lawrence. London: Chatto and Windus and New York: Oxford University Press, 1970.

Orwell (Modern Masters). London: Fontana/Collins and New York: Viking Press, 1971. Reprinted with postscript, London: Fontana Paperbacks, 1984.

The Country and the City. London: Chatto and Windus and New York: Oxford University Press, 1973.

Television: Technology and Cultural Form (Technosphere Series). London: Fontana, 1974; New York: Schocken, 1975.

Keywords: A Vocabulary of Culture and Society. London: Fontana/Croom Helm and New York: Oxford University Press, 1976. Revised edition, London: Fontana, 1983; New York: Oxford University Press, 1985.

Marxism and Literature (Marxist Introductions). London and New York: Oxford University Press, 1977.

Politics and Letters: Interviews with New Left Review. London: Verso Editions, and New York: Schocken, 1979.

Problems in Materialism and Culture: Selected Essays. London: Verso Editions, 1980; New York: Schocken, 1981.

Culture (Fontana New Sociology). London: Fontana, 1981. Published in America as *The Sociology of Culture.* New York: Schocken Books, 1982.

Cobbett (Past Masters). Oxford and New York: Oxford University Press, 1983.

Towards 2000. London: Chatto and Windus, The Hogarth Press, 1983. Published in America as *The Year Two Thousand.* New York: Pantheon Books, 1984.

Writing in Society. London: Verso Editions, 1983; New York: Schocken Books, 1984.

Critical Editions, Periodicals, Series

Editor, with Clifford Collins and Wolf Mankowitz, *Politics and Letters*, 1947–1948.

Editor, with Clifford Collins and Wolf Mankowitz, *The Critic*, 1947.

General Editor, *The New Thinker's Library.* London: C. A. Watts, 1962–1970.

Editor, with Stuart Hall and E. P. Thompson, *May-Day Manifesto 1968.* Harmondsworth: Penguin, 1968.

Editor, *The Pelican Book of English Prose: Volume 2: From 1780 to the*

Present Day. Harmondsworth: Penguin Books, 1969; Baltimore: Penguin Books, 1970.

Editor, with Joy Williams, *D. H. Lawrence on Education*. Harmondsworth: Penguin Books, 1973.

Editor, *George Orwell: A Collection of Critical Essays* (Twentieth Century Views). Englewood Cliffs, N.J.: Prentice-Hall, 1974.

General Editor, *Fontana Communications Series, 1976–1988*.

Editor, with Marie Axton, *English Drama: Forms and Development: Essays in Honour of Muriel Clara Bradbrook*. London: Cambridge University Press, 1977.

General Editor, with Steven Lukes, *Marxist Introductions*. London and New York: Oxford University Press, 1977–1988.

Editor, *Contact: Human Communication and Its History*. London and New York: Thames and Hudson, 1981.

Editor, *English Literature in History*. London: Hutchinson, 1983–1988.